PRAYERS

that avail much®

for DAILY LIVING

GERMAINE COPELAND

PRAYERS
that avail much®
for DAILY
LIVING

Charisma
HOUSE
A STRANG COMPANY

Most Strang Communications/Charisma House/Siloam products are available at special quantity discounts for bulk purchase for sales promotions, premiums, fund-raising, and educational needs. For details, write Strang Communications/Charisma House/Siloam, 600 Rinehart Road, Lake Mary, Florida 32746, or telephone (407) 333-0600.

Prayers That Avail Much® for Daily Living by Germaine Copeland
Published by Charisma House
A Strang Company
600 Rinehart Road
Lake Mary, Florida 32746
www.charismahouse.com

Unless otherwise noted, all Scripture quotations are from the New King James Version of the Bible. Copyright © 1979, 1980, 1982 by Thomas Nelson, Inc., publishers. Used by permission.

Scripture quotations marked AMP are from the Amplified Bible. Old Testament copyright © 1965, 1987 by the Zondervan Corporation. The Amplified New Testament copyright © 1954, 1958, 1987 by the Lockman Foundation. Used by permission.

Scripture quotations marked KJV are from the King James Version of the Bible.

Scripture quotations marked NASU are from the New American Standard Bible, updated Edition. Copyright © 1960, 1962, 1963, 1968, 1971, 1972, 1973, 1975, 1977, 1995 by the Lockman Foundation. Used by permission.

Scripture quotations marked NIV are from the Holy Bible, New International Version. Copyright © 1973, 1978, 1984, International Bible Society. Used by permission.

Scripture quotations marked NLT are from the Holy Bible, New Living Translation, copyright © 1996. Used by permission of Tyndale House Publishers, Inc., Wheaton, IL 60189. All rights reserved.

Scripture quotations marked THE MESSAGE are from *The Message: The Bible in Contemporary English*, copyright © 1993, 1994, 1995, 1996, 2000, 2001, 2002. Used by permission of NavPress Publishing Group.

Interior design by Terry Clifton

Library of Congress Cataloging-in-Publication Data:

Copeland, Germaine.
Prayers that avail much for daily living / Germaine Copeland.
   p. cm.
ISBN 1-59185-718-X (pbk.)
1. Prayer. 2. Prayers. I. Title.
BV210.3.C675 2005
242'.8--dc22

2004021474

First Edition

05 06 07 08 09 — 987654321

Printed in the United States of America

Contents

Introduction

Even though I loved my parents, I could hardly wait to grow up and leave the legalistic doctrines of my church. I grew up around a father who prepared sermons and always looked dapper when he left the house to visit his parishioners. He was intellectual, a student of the Bible, a pastor who followed all the rules of his denomination, and an austere father who ruled his family. His superiors and parishioners alike respected and loved him. You could count on him to do what he said he would do. Even though I hated the fanatical rules, he was my hero and I wanted to be like him.

My mother was a children's Sunday school teacher who prayed in the secrecy of her closet, kept the parsonage spotless, designed beautiful clothes, directed the choir, played the piano and organ, sang joyfully, and laughed with us. She was a woman of many talents. My parents prayed with us morning, noon, and night and made sure that we always looked our best for church.

Since I can remember, I've searched for the truth—a truth that would set me free. Because I had to live by what I considered to be unreasonably strict laws and regulations as the minister's daughter, I silently resisted the control and bondage that I viewed as my dream stealer. Everything fun was sin, and I lived with guilt and condemnation because I wanted to live outside the four walls of the church. The day came when I did leave the church, but guilt followed me. I worried that I might die and go to hell. It would be many years before I learned that God is a Father who loves us unconditionally.

When I began working in the big city, a whole new world opened up to me, and I could hardly wait to experience life. But nothing prepared me to live outside the confines of my denomination, and I suffered unidentified fears that left me paralyzed.

I was faced with a new dream stealer. Sometimes I would overcome fear for a season and believe that with each new adventure my life would be different. The fear that I could never measure up, never be good enough, always came back with greater intensity. Getting married and having four children proved my greatest fear: I was a failure and a mistake. The freedom that I sought was beyond my reach.

BUT GOD! I love the "but God" in the Bible. The One who chose me before the foundation of the world visited me, and He never left. Those years of living with a father who studied the Bible and a mother who prayed found a home in my heart and mind—"Train up a child in the way [s]he should go, and when [s]he is old [s]he will not depart from it" (Prov. 22:6).

Day by day my soul began a transformation that continues today. My crippled emotions were healed, and my needs were met. I resolved issues that had been the true dream stealers of my life.

Through daily communion with God, writing, praying scriptural prayers, and listening for His voice, the strongholds that protected my crippled emotions came tumbling down. My life was changed one day at a time. My soul was restored, my marriage was healed, our son was delivered from addictions, and our daughters are walking paths of righteousness. God has done great things!

Most of the teachings, short stories, and real life experiences that I am sharing here are from the pages of my personal journal. You will be inspired and will come into a deeper, more intimate relationship with the Father who satisfies your soul and loves you with an everlasting love. God is love. You are born of love, and when you abide in Him and His words abide in you, you shall ask what you will and it will be done.

Prayer is the secret that unlocks the heart of the Father.

Day 1

A Prayer for the New Year

Daily Scripture Verse

Watch and pray, lest you enter into temptation. The spirit indeed is willing, but the flesh is weak.

—MARK 14:38

Daily Prayer

Heavenly Father, thank You for giving me a fresh start. Your Word holds first place in my life. I purpose to keep Your thoughts ever in mind. Your words are penetrating deep into my heart, for they are real life and radiant health for me. You are my exceeding great joy, and this year I will have joy that drives away gloom. With Your divine energy, I will learn the skill of living the more abundant life.

Just as a tree branch turns to the sun, I am reaching and stretching toward You, the Son who rose with healing in His wings. I am a branch grafted into the Vine, and the life of God flows through me. Thank You for giving me understanding about what You want me to do and making me wise about spiritual things.

Your Word is streamlining my goals according to Your plans and purposes. Thank You for new relationships and new connections that You will bring forth with Your mighty power. My primary goal is to know You better so our relationship will become even stronger this year. My belief is in victory, not defeat. Success will come to me as I seek first Your kingdom and Your righteousness (Your way of doing and being right). Forgetting the past, I look forward to what lies ahead.

Father, I thank You for sending Jesus that I might have life and have it more abundantly. Help me remember that my relationships with You and with others are more important than anything else. Father, I make Your Word my compass, and my life is complete in Christ. I purpose to cast all my cares, worries, and concerns over on You, that I might be well balanced (temperate, sober of mind), vigilant, and cautious at all times. Thank You for watching over Your Word to perform it in my life, in the name of Jesus. Amen.

Day 2

Commit to Read God's Word

Daily Scripture Verse

I will meditate on Your precepts,
And contemplate Your ways.
I will delight myself in Your statutes;
I will not forget Your Word.

—Psalm 119:15–16

It is early morning, and a hush is in the air. Gazing at the pink glow of the sky, I breathe deeply. My soul is restored as I silently behold the rosy, pink light reflected in the lake. If only I could capture this moment in time—so peaceful and holy. Then I realize this peace and holiness is the constant, indwelling presence of God.

In the consuming quietness I wait on the Lord in contemplative prayer. Just as my cup of joy is overflowing, I hear a still, small voice saying, "I want you to make your schedule around My Word. Read it from cover to cover in the Amplified Bible."

Immediately I protest, "Father, let me read another version. The Amplified has so many extra words."

Have you noticed how patient He is with us? "You have eternity," He says. The resistance falls away, and I make a commitment to myself—I will read the Amplified Bible through this year.

Put first things first, and pause for a while. Spend time in the presence of the Father. Seek His plans for your life. You will never be happier than when you choose to follow Him. "Lord, I ask You to direct my entire study program for this year, the discipline You would have me follow that I might become more like Jesus."

> All Scripture is given by inspiration of God, and is profitable for doctrine, for reproof, for correction, for instruction in righteousness, that the man of God may be complete, thoroughly equipped for every good work.
>
> —2 Timothy 3:16–17

Daily Prayer

> *Father, I exalt Your Word, hold it in high esteem, and give it first place in my schedule. I agree with the Word of God, and I cast down any thoughts, imaginations, and/ or reasoning contrary to Your Word. The Word is the final authority in all my deliberations. Boldly and confidently I say that my heart is fixed and established on the solid foundation—the Word of God! Amen.*

Day 3

Begin the Repair Work

Daily Scripture Verse

> Those from among you
> Shall build the old waste places;
> You shall raise up the foundations of many
>   generations;
> And you shall be called the Repairer of the Breach,
> The Restorer of Streets to Dwell In.
>
> —Isaiah 58:12

*C*hristmas decorations had been taken down and put away, and the bare tree looking forlorn and forsaken was at the curb to be picked up. Life was returning to its normal routine, and it was time to get back to the office. Hopefully, all the loose ends of last year were tied up and ready to be stored in the archive boxes. If only our relationships could be as neatly sorted out and cataloged.

Reliving again the terrible scene at the end of the family Christmas get-together, I prayed for wisdom. "God, I cannot change anyone else. I remember when You spoke to me by Your Holy Spirit saying that I would see a miracle of love in my family. I will hold this word in my heart. Father, I ask You for wisdom that I might know how to build the old waste places and raise up the foundations of many generations. I would be a repairer of the breach, a restorer of paths to dwell in" (Isa. 58:12).

Since the fall of Adam and Eve, families have appeared dysfunctional. In spite of this, God's plan unfolded. I am encouraged when I remember the reconciliation of Jacob and Esau, brothers who did not see each other for many years. One of Jacob's sons,

Joseph, was present on this monumental day, and he would later experience alienation and reconciliation in his generation. God is looking for one person who will be the one to reverse long-standing pain and alienation in each family.

In 2 Chronicles 7:14, God promised, "If My people who are called by My name will humble themselves, and pray and seek My face, and turn from their wicked ways, then I will hear from heaven, and will forgive their sin and heal their land." The *land* begins with *our families*. God's mercy will triumph over judgment. He will forgive; He will heal family relationships. He is not a man that He should lie. Stand on the promises of God; commit your ways to Him. You and your household shall be saved.

> Now all things are of God, who has reconciled us to Himself through Jesus Christ, and has given us the ministry of reconciliation.
>
> —2 Corinthians 5:18

Daily Prayer

> *Father, in the name of Jesus, we are abiding in the Vine, and He abides in us to bring to our lives a harvest of love, joy, peace, forbearance, kindness, benevolence, meekness, and self-restraint. We belong to Christ, having nailed our natural evil desires to His cross and crucified them there. Father, we are not desirous of vainglory and will not provoke or envy one another, but we seek to bring forth those good fruits to the praise and glory of God. Amen.*

Day 4

One Day at a Time

Daily Scripture Verse

> Then the LORD answered me and said:
> "Write the vision
> And make it plain on tablets,
> That he may run who reads it.
> For the vision is yet for an appointed time;
> But at the end it will speak, and it will not lie.
> Though it tarries, wait for it;
> Because it will surely come,
> It will not tarry."
>
> —HABAKKUK 2:2–3

Traditionally, Sue looked forward to new beginnings, but the past year had been difficult. Discouragement settled over her like a wet blanket. Sitting at the kitchen table, she stared at the blank page in her new journal wondering where to begin. So many prayers unanswered; goals of the previous year were unfulfilled. Yet, she welcomed the year that stretched before her like a book waiting to be written.

Grieving over the unresolved issues that erupted at the family gathering over the holidays, she wondered where she had failed. Silently, she bowed her head, asking her Father to revitalize her hope and renew the vision for the salvation of her children and grandchildren.

Putting the pen to the paper she began writing her God-given desires and goals, many the same as last year. She would take it one day at a time. Surely, the vision will come to pass; the Word was her surety that her family would be saved.

Believe on the Lord Jesus Christ, and you will be saved, you and your household.

—ACTS 16:31

Daily Prayer

Father, I will wait upon You and order my conversation aright. I will see Your salvation revealed in my family. I need Your wisdom as I walk through this day—at home and at work—in all my relationships one day at a time. You caused Jesus to be made wisdom unto me; He is my patience, and Your timing is perfect. Holy Spirit, remind me that the fear of the Lord is wisdom and to depart from evil is understanding. I reverence You, my Lord, and depart from evil. Thank You for Your gift of wisdom that is from above. Help me remember that it is first pure, then peaceable, gentle, and easy to be entreated, full of mercy and good fruits, without partiality, and without hypocrisy. Amen.

Day 5

Letting Go of Yesterday

Daily Scripture Verse

Now we look inside, and what we see is that anyone united with the Messiah gets a fresh start, is created new. The old life is gone; a new life burgeons! Look at it! All this comes from the God who settled the relationship between us and him, and then called us to settle our relationships with each other.

—2 CORINTHIANS 5:17–18, THE MESSAGE

*H*ere we are. Another new year—a new beginning. In Christ new beginnings are limitless. We can begin each day with expectancy. I may not be all that I want to be today, but I am not what I used to be. Tomorrow I will not be the same as I am today. I expect to be different, transformed by the Spirit of God.

My dad, Rev. Buck Griffin, awoke every morning with great expectations. He affirmed every day that old things of yesterday were passed away; today everything is brand-new. Letting go of yesterday with its mistakes and failures prepares us to become more deeply and intimately acquainted with the eternal God. You can know Him through His written Word and by prayer. Hanging on to yesterday is not worth the magnificent opportunity we would miss.

God is the architect and builder of this wondrous universe. He is big enough to measure the waters in the hollow of his hand, to mark off the heavens with the span of His hand, and enclose the dust of the earth in a measure. He weighed the mountains in scales and the hills in a balance (Isa. 40:12). Yet, He is small enough to live in the heart of a child.

Because He lives in your heart, you can let go of the past even though it may have been difficult. Trust God to cause all things to work together for your good. (See Romans 8:28.) Receive the ministry of reconciliation, and reach out to others. Let's remember that a smile can speak to the heart of another; that a calm, gentle spirit can still turbulent waters, overcoming an atmosphere of chaos and unrest; and that our words can heal those who are hurting and looking for answers. Allow God's Word to change you, share His love with others, and make a commitment to honor Him. When you are tempted to react negatively to situations, remember the Holy Spirit is present to help you and to give you the soft answer that turns away wrath.

Practice God's awesome presence every moment of every day, and submit to the constant ministry of transformation by the Holy Spirit!

> You will show me the path of life;
> In Your presence is fullness of joy;
> At Your right hand are pleasures forevermore.
> —Psalm 16:11

Daily Prayer

> *Our Father who is in heaven, I delight myself in You and thank You for another new year. I let go of the past with its mistakes, hurts, and disappointment. I pray that Christ will be more and more at home in my heart, living within me as I trust in Him. May my roots go down deep into the soil of Your marvelous love. May I be able to feel and understand, with all God's children, how long, how wide, how deep, and how high Your love really is. May I be able to experience this love for myself, though it is so great that I will never see the end of it or fully know or understand it. And so at last I will be filled with God Himself. Amen.*

Day 1

The Word Becomes Life

Daily Scripture Verse

> If you remain in me and my words remain in you, ask
> whatever you wish, and it will be given you.
>
> —JOHN 15:7, NIV

In the midst of my desperation, God came to my kitchen. I
was drawn to unconditional love like a moth drawn to the
light. The Creator filled my entire being with an insatiable desire to read the Bible. Picking up the only Bible I could find, I
read *Good News for Modern Man* from cover to cover. God's
Word became my life. Taking my S&H Green Stamps, I bought
a white King James Version of the Bible with Old and New tes-
taments. Day and night I attended to God's Word, consented
and submitted to His sayings. The Word became my constant
companion. I read in my car while waiting for my children to
complete music lessons, ball, or cheerleading practice. I propped
the Bible up on the kitchen counter in front of me when I ironed,
held it in my hand while vacuuming—memorizing scriptures. If
only I could print it on my mind and my heart.

I could see where I was going; His Word became a shining
light in a dark world, and the darkness could not put it out. His
Word became my life, and my life would never be the same.

Daily Prayer

> *Father, in the name of Jesus, I purpose to read, medi-*
> *tate, and walk in Your Word daily. Your Word living*
> *in me lights my pathway, making my way plain before*
> *me. Thank You for keeping me steady and helping me*
> *to keep first things first, because Your Word is steadfast,*

sure, and eternal. I trust my everyday life and my family to its provisions. Your words were found, and I did eat them; they are the rejoicing of my heart. I will not stumble, for my steps are ordered in the Word.

Day 2

A Field Under Cultivation

Daily Scripture Verse

> …that Christ may dwell in your hearts through faith; that you, being rooted and grounded in love, may be able to comprehend with all the saints what is the width and length and depth and height—to know the love of Christ which passes knowledge; that you may be filled with all the fullness of God.
>
> —Ephesians 3:17–19

The sky was clear blue with soft clouds floating about, and the gentle breeze played a pleasing tune on the wind chimes. Enjoying the gentle motion of the white wicker swing, I took a deep breath and closed my eyes. An old nursery rhyme interrupted my thoughts, "Mary, Mary, quite contrary, how does your garden grow?" Puzzled, I wondered how I could answer this question, which refused to go away. Did this apply to me?

Awake, but not awake, I viewed a brown, dry, crusted-over field that seemed to have no beginning and no ending. This was no garden. This didn't look like ground fit for flower or vegetable. I gazed at the earth that lay there producing nothing.

Then I saw a figure emerging on the horizon of the vast garden plot. With eyes closed, I watched Him as He began to move. To my amazement, He was plowing up the fallow ground.

As I le drew nearer, I recognized the Holy Spirit, who was whistling a happy tune.

Somehow I knew that He was plowing up my heart. Tears of gratitude gushed from my eyes, splashing onto the front of my blouse. I watched the Holy Spirit turn furrow after furrow into moist, fertile earth.

In simple humility, I waited. A desire to read God's Word arose, and day by day my gardener continues to landscape me with seed from the Word, making a salvation garden of my life.

> He who received seed on the good ground is he who hears the word and understands it, who indeed bears fruit and produces: some a hundredfold, some sixty, some thirty.
>
> —MATTHEW 13:23

Daily Prayer

Father, I acknowledge You as my God. You called me to be a fellow workman (joint promoter, laborer together) with and for You. I am Your field under cultivation. Thank You for breaking up the fallow ground of my heart for the planting of the Word. I will sow to myself in righteousness, reap in mercy, and seek You 'til You come and rain righteousness upon me. My heart is well-adapted soil, and I have ears to hear Your Word. I receive, accept, and welcome it. I will bear fruit to Your glory…a hundred times as much as was sown. Amen.

Day 3

The Power of Praying the Word

Daily Scripture Verse

> Now this is the confidence that we have in Him, that if
> we ask anything according to His will, He hears us. And
> if we know that He hears us, whatever we ask, we know
> that we have the petitions that we have asked of Him.
>
> —1 John 5:14–15

The Master Creator, the God of the universe, wants to walk with you and talk with you. He has given you a language that is creative and powerful enough to open the heavens and release His glory, His majesty. Nothing that occurs on your journey through life comes as a surprise to your heavenly Father. He uses everything to complete His work that He has begun in you. You are His masterpiece!

God sent the Holy Spirit to you. He not only walks with you, but He also abides in you. When you have done all you know to do and feel like giving up, the Holy Spirit is present to strengthen you. When your faith seems exhausted, He activates the faith of the Son of God that abides in you. He lifts you up. He leads you into a place of rest and peace that passes understanding. He never leaves you without support. He gives you the courage to approach a holy God who is present to hear you when you pray.

How can you know God's will? His Word is His will, and if His Word abides in you and you abide in Him, you can ask what you desire and it shall be done for you. (See John 15:7.)

When your enemy would have you believe that you are insignificant, the Word of God is powerful enough to expose misbeliefs about who you are. Your life is significant, you are

chosen by God to be His very own, and you are the righteousness of God in Christ Jesus. Depression, self pity, and fear lie to you, but God gives you the courage to overcome. The Word of God is hope, the Word of God is health, and the Word of God assures you that the sun will rise again.

The Word of God is not just words written on a page or a history book. His Word is so powerful and creative that the universe with its planets, sun, moon, and stars was framed by it. The Word of God is creative and is still creating today.

> By faith we understand that the worlds were framed by the word of God, so that the things which are seen were not made of things which are visible.
>
> —HEBREWS 11:3

Daily Prayer

> *Father, my delight is in the law of the Lord; in Your law I meditate day and night. I am like a tree planted by streams of water, which yields its fruit in season and whose leaf does not wither. Whatever I do prospers. Thank You for Your Word that goes out from Your mouth: it will not return to You empty, but it will accomplish what You desire and achieve the purpose for which You sent it. I submit to Your Word and will speak words of life, in the name of Jesus. Amen.*

Day 4

Benefits of Praying God's Word

Daily Scripture Verse

> Your word I have hidden in my heart,
> That I might not sin against You!…

I will meditate on Your precepts,
And contemplate Your ways.
I will delight myself in Your statutes;
I will not forget Your word.

—PSALM 119:11, 15–16

*P*raying the Word is powerful and rewarding. God watches over His Word to perform it. Faith comes by hearing, and hearing by the Word. God speaks to your heart from the pages of His written Word, and He also speaks to your inner being in a quiet voice. His voice and His Word agree. When you pray scriptural prayers aloud, you are speaking and hearing the Word. You can pray prayers that avail much.

At times, it seems God is feeding thoughts into your mind. You see, you are a partaker of His divine nature. And as you spend more time with Him, you become more like Him, conformed into the image of His dear Son by the Spirit of God.

Prayer is not mystical, but practical and purposeful. Prayer is a spiritual business with written laws that govern the affairs of life. Prayer consists of different forms of supplication and entreaty.

As believers, we are to be alert and watch with strong purpose. Our purpose is to enforce the triumphant victory of our Lord Jesus Christ here on earth. We do that as we continually pray, "Father, Your will be done on earth as it is in heaven."

So don't ever give up; keep on persevering. The Holy Spirit is practical, and He leads you into the reality of all realities in the spirit.

Praying scriptural prayers will change you from the inside out. Praying God's Word, which is truth, will cause you to become more willing to face the realities of life and deal with the truth about yourself and your relationships. It will also help you grow in the grace and knowledge of our Lord Jesus Christ.

As you replace your old thought patterns with God's thoughts, even your behavior will change. You will be transformed from the inside out, and others will see Jesus in you!

> Grace and peace be multiplied to you in the knowledge of God and of Jesus our Lord…by which have been given to us exceedingly great and precious promises, that through these you may be partakers of the divine nature.
>
> —2 PETER 1:2, 4

Daily Prayer

Father, in the name of Jesus, I make a commitment to You and to myself to walk in the Word. Your Word living in me produces Your life in this world. I recognize that Your Word is integrity itself—steadfast, sure, eternal—and I trust my life to its provisions. By the power of the Holy Spirit Your Word dwells in me richly in all wisdom. I meditate on it day and night so that I may diligently act on it, and bring glory to Your name. Amen.[1]

Day 5

The Word Is Your Weapon

Daily Scripture Verse

> For the word of God is living and powerful, and sharper than any two-edged sword, piercing even to the division of soul and spirit, and of joints and marrow, and is a discerner of the thoughts and intents of the heart.
>
> —HEBREWS 4:12

You are using a spiritual weapon when you speak the Word of God into and over your God-given prayer assignments. The Word of God is a quick, sharp, powerful weapon that divides light and darkness.

When you speak in agreement with God's Word concerning those things that concern you, your words are spirit and life. In John 6:63 Jesus said that the Spirit gives life; the flesh counts for nothing. The words that He spoke were spirit and life. When you pray scriptural prayers, you are speaking the Word of God (His will) as revealed by His Son, Jesus Christ. His words become your words, releasing the power of God to do above and beyond anything you ask. When you pray scriptural prayers, you are speaking words that are spirit and life; your faith is increased. Scriptural prayers are quick (alive) powerful, and sharper than any double-edged sword.

Jesus is the Way, the Truth, and the Life. All authority of heaven and earth has been given to Jesus, the head of the body, and you are a joint heir with Him. When you pray His Word of Truth, your words carry the weight of the authority of His kingdom, His Word, and His unchangeable promises.

The Word of Truth that is near you, in your mouth, and in your heart is powerful and unchanging. The Holy Spirit helps you to pray when you pray in agreement with Jesus. He and Jesus are two powerful intercessors who cannot fail! God watches over His Word to perform it. His Word will never wither or fade away. God's Word is sure and stands forever! He had men write His thoughts and His ways so that you can learn His ways and how He thinks. The more you learn about God, the more you will trust Him, and the more you will love Him because He first loved you.

God hears you, and God will answer your prayer according to His will, His purpose, and His plan for you!

God…has saved us and called us with a holy calling, not according to our works, but according to His own purpose and grace.

—2 TIMOTHY 1:8–9

Daily Prayer

As the rain and the snow come down from heaven and do not return to it without watering the earth and making it bud and flourish so that the earth yields seed for the sower and bread for the eater, so is God's Word that goes out from His mouth. When He speaks, and when I speak His Word, it will not return empty, but it will accomplish what I desire and achieve the purpose for which I sent it. Father, I thank You for creating in me Your desires. Amen.

Day 1

A Lifestyle of Prayer

Daily Scripture Verse

I bow my knees to the Father of our Lord Jesus Christ, from whom the whole family in heaven and earth is named, that He would grant you, according to the riches of His glory, to be strengthened with might through His Spirit in the inner man.

—EPHESIANS 3:14–16

There has been needless fallout in the body of Christ because of a lack of sound teaching on the lifestyle of prayer. In the first three chapters of Ephesians, Paul reveals the secrets that God has imparted to us. He explains in detail the spiritual blessings God has given us—our redemption, who we are in Christ, and the supremacy of Jesus. He prays for us to have wisdom and revelation knowledge. Power to live victoriously, regardless of circumstances, has been imparted to the believer. By grace through faith we have been saved and made to sit together in heavenly places in Christ Jesus.

We are the body of Christ and are being built together for a dwelling place of God in the Spirit. Paul reveals that Christ will dwell in our hearts, and we will be rooted and grounded in love. If we develop a lifestyle of prayer, we will discover that it is possible to comprehend the love of Christ and to be filled with all the fullness of God!

God has given us everything we need to enforce the triumphant victory Jesus won at Calvary. We have been made victorious over the evil one. We can access all the power and authority of God by developing a life that is committed to prayer—our entrance into the throne room of God.

...that Christ may dwell in your hearts through faith; that you, being rooted and grounded in love may be able to comprehend with all the saints what is the width and length and depth and height—to know the love of Christ which passes knowledge; that you may be filled with all the fullness of God.

—EPHESIANS 3:17–19

Daily Prayer

Father, in the name of Jesus, I am Your building under construction—a house of prayer. I abide in You, and Your Word abides in me. With the Holy Spirit as my helper, and by the grace of God, I commit to a life of prayer—I will not turn coward or give up. I desire to become more deeply and intimately acquainted with You, my Father, my Lord and Savior Jesus Christ. Amen.

Day 2

Prayer Is Our Contact With God

Daily Scripture Verse

Behold, I will do a new thing,
Now it shall spring forth;
Shall you not know it?
I will even make a way in the wilderness
And rivers in the desert.

—ISAIAH 43:19

It was during a time of great spiritual drought that God created in me a desire to read the Scriptures. The Bible became my constant companion and prayer book; I couldn't

read enough or fast enough. My entire being cried out, "Let me know and pursue the knowledge of the Lord." His going forth is established as the morning. He will come to me like the rain, like the latter and former rain to the earth. (See Hosea 6:3.)

A new day dawned, and my life was changed. I had a reason to live! My wilderness was made glad as the desert places of my life blossomed as a rose. I rejoiced with joy and singing. I beheld the glory of the Lord and the excellency of my God!

A relationship was born that day—a relationship that has grown deeper and more intimate with passing days. Jesus is my Lord, God is my Father, and the Holy Spirit is my Teacher.

Prayer is a lifestyle, not a ritual. The Bible is God's voice speaking to us, and prayer is our contact with Him. Daily conversation with God is a heavenly privilege available to every believer. The Father has reserved divine secrets for His children, and prayer is the key that unlocks the door of His storehouse.

Once we were children of darkness; now we are children of light. As partakers of the nature of God, we are receptive to the light and have the spiritual capacity to comprehend and understand God's thoughts and God's ways, which are higher than ours.

As I read, prayerfully meditating on His Word, my path grows brighter and brighter: chaos turns to order, mysteries are unveiled, enigmas unravel, and God's plan for my life continues to unfold. A new beginning—another new day is dawning.

> The secret things belong to the Lord our God, but those things which are revealed belong to us and to our children forever, that we may do all the words of this law.
>
> —Deuteronomy 29:29

Father of glory, I ask You to grant me a spirit of wisdom and revelation [of insight into mysteries and secrets] in the [deep and intimate] knowledge of the Lord Jesus Christ. Flood the eyes of my heart with light, so that I can know and understand the hope to which You have called me. I praise You and thank You for hearing my prayer, in the name of Jesus, my soon coming King. Amen.

Day 3

Prayer Is Positive Confession

Daily Scripture Verse

Whenever I am afraid,
I will trust in You.

—Psalm 56:3

On the edge of a cliff was a magnificent Ferris wheel. Lynn and her mom decided to ride together. They were laughing and having fun as they ascended higher and higher.

All of a sudden the Ferris wheel stopped. They were stuck at the very top! The beauty of the peaks, sky, and valleys faded, and Lynn was terrified. With every second and sway of the cart, she became more and more afraid.

The fear was overpowering. Lynn gripped the bar in front of her tighter and tighter. With a loving embrace, her mom put her arm around her, praying, "Father, in the name of Jesus, whenever we are afraid we will trust in You. Perfect love casts out fear." Her mom encouraged Lynn to repeat the prayer after her. Lynn's trembling voice gave way to strength and courage as she prayed aloud. After several minutes Lynn relaxed and

said, "Mommy, I'm not afraid any more." As Lynn was released from her fear, the grinding of gears began, and the Ferris wheel moved. Everyone arrived safely on the ground.

By faith the prayer of positive confession drove away Lynn's fear. You can overcome those things in life that seem insurmountable. God has given you the gift of His Word to use in every area of your life. When you pray God's Word, you are praying with power.

> There is no fear in love; but perfect love casts out fear.
> —1 John 4:18

Daily Prayer

> *The joy of the Lord is my strength. The Lord is my rock, and my fortress, and my deliverer; my God, my strength, in whom I will trust; my buckler, and the horn of my salvation, and my high tower. You fill me with strength and protect me wherever I go.*
>
> *I stagger not at the promise of God through unbelief; but I am strong in faith, giving glory to God—strong in the Lord and in His mighty power. Jesus is Lord over my spirit, soul, and body. Amen.*

Day 4

A Word to Parents

Daily Scripture Verse

> Therefore you shall lay up these words of mine in your heart and in your soul, and…you shall teach them to your children, speaking of them when you sit in your

house, when you walk by the way, when you lie down, and when you rise up.

—DEUTERONOMY 11:18–19

*P*arents, you probably have the most challenging of jobs—building and developing godly character in the lives of your children, training each child in the way he or she is to go. Your children are tomorrow's leaders: presidents, ministers, educators, inventors, and developers of new technology.

In today's society this responsibility has become increasingly more difficult as many mothers, some who are single, have full-time jobs outside the home. In addition we must face issues of the threat of violence in our schools, the pressure of "keeping up with the Joneses," and the rising cost of education, just to name a few. Family, friends, peers, the media, and caregivers who may not have your same values influence your children.

So, how can you stay strengthened amid all the pressures? How do you overcome worry and fear? How do you mold the lives of your children as caring, loving individuals and establish them in their walk with God? These questions demand answers and become more significant with each passing year. Parents from past generations have wanted answers to these same perplexing enigmas.

The solution is wrapped up in one powerful word—*prayer*. The Father is always available to heal wounded spirits, to give comfort, wisdom, and strength. Take time each morning to wait before the Lord in prayer, to read the Bible, and to meditate. Fifteen minutes will strengthen you. In the midst of unpleasant situations, pause, acknowledge the presence of God, take a few deep breaths, and you will change the atmosphere. A silent prayer will place you in a position to hear from God, and He will direct your path. He is your patience, your unseen partner

as you teach and train your children in the ways of God. If God be for you, who can be against you?

> Train up a child in the way he should go,
> And when he is old he will not depart from it.
>
> —PROVERBS 22:6

Daily Prayer

> *Heavenly Father, I commit myself, as a parent, to train my child/children in the way he is to go, trusting in Your promise that he will not depart from Your ways, but will grow and prosper in them. I turn the care and burden of rearing him over to You. I purpose to nurture and love him as You have loved us. I will command and teach my child diligently. Your grace is sufficient to overcome my weaknesses as a mother/father. Amen.*

Day 5

An Open Invitation

Daily Scripture Verse

> Let us therefore come boldly to the throne of grace, that we may obtain mercy and find grace to help in time of need.
>
> —HEBREWS 4:16

*A*s my daughter and her family arrive from their distant abode in Florida, my husband and I rush outside smiling and waving. The car doors open, the grandchildren, without hesitation, boldly jump out of the van except for the sleepy one that isn't quiet awake yet. They run first into their granddaddy's open arms, and one by one he swoops them up and swings them

above his head. Joyously they reach for the sky. Even the little one in her mother's arms looks up with contentment. They are home with Nonna and Granddaddy.

The grandchildren see their grandfather as a person who is worthy of trust. He plays with them, and they follow him around, sometimes pouting when he has to say no. But in a few moments they are at ease knowing that someone is lovingly setting boundaries. Feeling safe, they scamper away to bring out the toys or get treats from the kitchen.

God is eagerly searching the horizon to see if He can catch a glimpse of you. Prayer is your approach to God. He wants to see your face and hear your voice. Come with a trusting heart, knowing that He will receive you. Come confidently and boldly, taking your place as His child. He made you and redeemed you. Acknowledge Him as your Father. Wherever you are, you have freedom to enter into the holy of holies by the blood of the Lamb. Just speak the name of Jesus.

Jesus is asking, "Are you tired? Worn out? Burned out on religion? Come to me. Get away with me, and you'll recover your life. I'll show you how to take a real rest" (Matt. 11:28, The Message). Jesus wants you to know Him. To know Him is to know the Father. If you refuse to come, He doesn't give up on you. Look! He has been standing at the door, constantly knocking. If you hear Him calling, open the door. He will come in and fellowship with you.

> Behold, I stand at the door and knock. If anyone hears
> My voice and opens the door, I will come in to him and
> dine with him, and he with Me.
> —Revelation 3:20

Daily Prayer

Father, in the name of Jesus, I will not draw back or shrink in fear, for then Your soul would have no delight or pleasure in me. I was bought for a price—purchased with preciousness and paid for, made Your very own. I honor You, Lord, and desire to bring glory to You in my body. I will let my light shine before men that they may see my moral excellence and praiseworthy good deeds, that they may recognize, honor, praise, and glorify You, my Father who is in heaven. Amen.

Day 1

Come Into His Presence

Daily Scripture Verse

Hear my prayer, O Lᴏʀᴅ,
And let my cry come to You.
Do not hide Your face from me in the day of my
trouble;
Incline Your ear to me;
In the day that I call, answer me speedily.

—Psᴀʟᴍ 102:1–2

God is calling you into the sweet communion and fellowship of the Holy Spirit. He is concerned with everything that concerns you. You can speak frankly, openly, and honestly to Him in your everyday language. You don't have to speak eloquently, but simply and plainly.

Sometimes I talk with Christians who are uncomfortable in God's presence. The way you overcome this feeling is by developing your relationship with Him through Bible reading, meditation, and prayer. Get rid of your misbeliefs, and renew your mind to the Word of God. Today, you are a son or daughter of God—a God who sees, a God who hears you when you pray.

If you have sinned, don't hide as Adam did in the Garden of Eden, but run to Him; receive His mercy and forgiveness. Receive His gift of grace. Receive the ability to take your place as His very own son or daughter. He isn't like any earthly dad; He is sufficient to supply all that you need.

You belong here in the throne room in your Father's presence. You are His child. You will find mercy and grace to help you in your time of need. His mercies are new every morning, and He lavishly heaps grace and more grace upon you, even

more than you are able to receive. Come into His presence; recognize and know that He is your God. He is not withholding any good thing from you. This mighty God is your Friend, Redeemer, Counselor, Prince of Peace, and your loving Father who will never leave you or forsake you. Here in His presence is fullness of joy, your strength for the day. Having come confidently and boldly to the throne of grace, you can go out knowing that you are never alone. God's presence goes with you.

> Through the LORD's mercies we are not consumed,
> Because His compassions fail not.
> They are new every morning;
> Great is Your faithfulness.
>
> —LAMENTATIONS 3:22–23

Daily Prayer

Father, I come before You rejoicing, for this is the day that You have made, and I will be glad in it. To obey is better than sacrifice, so I am making a decision to submit to Your will today, that my plans and purposes may be conducted in a manner that will bring honor and glory to You. Cause me to be spiritually and mentally alert in this time of meditation and prayer, in the name of Jesus. Amen.

Day 2

Desire to Pray

Daily Scripture Verse

The effective, fervent prayer of a righteous man avails much.

—JAMES 5:16

$\mathcal{M}$ ore and more people are seeking effective methods to relieve the stress and strain of today's hectic lifestyles. Violence erupts in places where we once felt safe, and increasingly, people are turning to prayer. All over the world, in all cultures and throughout time, people have prayed either to false gods or to the God of Abraham, Isaac, and Jacob. God intended for spiritual truths to be passed down from generation to generation, but today, even in our churches, many have lost the art of prayer.

How can you know that you are righteous? If you are a Christian you are a new person, and you have been made right with God through Christ. This gives you the right to come into the presence of God just as you are. You come in the name of Jesus, and God answers prayer because He is good. God draws you to Himself with cords of love.

A need to pray may have been tugging at your heart, but the desire to pray often begins at your point of need. God meets you where you are and delegates His grace on your behalf. He is calling you to be an agent of the Lord Jesus Christ, and when you answer, "Here I am, Lord," you are in the school of prayer. Your textbook is the Bible, and the Holy Spirit is your instructor. Learning to pray requires on-the-job training. You pray, and God begins the process of revealing Himself to you. You receive spiritual wisdom and understanding so that you might grow in the grace and knowledge of Jesus Christ. The eyes of your understanding are enlightened so that you can understand the greatness of His power to the believer. As you continue training, practicing prayer, your confidence in God is strengthened.

You are unique, and your development is unique. The lifestyle of prayer can be learned from others who share their experiences and teachings. In my experience the Holy Spirit led me from one phase of prayer to another. Everyone is called to pray,

and together we stand shoulder to shoulder in orderly array—for God, and against the forces of darkness.

> Therefore I also…do not cease to give thanks for you, making mention of you in my prayers: that…the eyes of your understanding being enlightened; that you may know what is the hope of His calling, what are the riches of the glory of His inheritance in the saints.
>
> —EPHESIANS 1:15–18

Daily Prayer

> *In the name of Jesus, I resist the temptation to be anxious about anything, but in every circumstance and in everything, by prayer and petition [definite requests] with thanksgiving, I will continue to make my wants known to God. Whatever I ask for in prayer, I believe that it is granted to me, and I shall receive it to the glory of the Father. Amen.*

Day 3

Commit to Prayer

Daily Scripture Verse

> Rejoice always, pray without ceasing, in everything give thanks; for this is the will of God in Christ Jesus for you.
>
> —1 THESSALONIANS 5:16–18

Prayer is relationship. I remember the early days of euphoria when I valued, above everything, time alone with God, and nothing could stand in my way. It was a repeat of the early days of my marriage when I couldn't wait for my husband

to come home. As the years progressed, the compulsion to be together waned, and we had to purpose to spend time together. You may be weary in your prayer life and wondering why the zeal and enthusiasm you once felt have abated. Perhaps you have found yourself in turmoil.

Out of this inner conflict you take another step of faith. When you have tasted the good things of God, you are unwilling to return to your former spiritual state. Jesus said that we are to pray without ceasing. He is bringing you up to another level –the level of commitment. You have the opportunity to make the commitment to pray and not give up. This is one of the first lessons in the school of prayer.

God doesn't force anyone to do anything. How do we overcome times of dryness and spiritual apathy? Praying in the Spirit and reading the Scriptures in prayer form will stir up your desire to pray. You may pray from the Book of Ephesians:

> Blessed be the God and Father of our Lord Jesus Christ, who has blessed us with every spiritual blessing in the heavenly places in Christ.
>
> —EPHESIANS 1:3

Daily Prayer

> *Father of glory, thank You for blessing me with every spiritual blessing in the heavenly realms because I belong to Christ. You chose me before the foundation of the world to be holy and without blame before You in love. You purchased my freedom through the blood of Your Son, and my sins are forgiven. Now, Father, I pray that my heart will be flooded with light so that I can understand the wonderful future You have promised.*

Day 4

Persevere in Your Praying

Daily Scripture Verse

> Let us not grow weary while doing good, for in due
> season we shall reap if we do not lose heart.
>
> —GALATIANS 6:9

*M*aking a commitment to pray is the first step. Perseverance will follow. You are not alone. The Holy Spirit
is present to help you. When you are tempted to grow weary
of doing good, encourage yourself in the Lord. Do not give up,
for you will reap a harvest of blessing at the appropriate time.

In the beginning of my walk with God, my quiet times
could have been called "get-acquainted coffees" with God. I
read His Word aloud, He talked with me, and I talked with
Him. The highest form of worship is the study of God's
Word.

From Genesis to Revelation men and women talked with
God. The Old Testament prophets had no guidebooks to teach
them the art of prayer. Many of their prayers are recorded, and
their examples of faith and courage inspire us to go from glory
to glory, faith to faith. The Old Testament prayers were not
always sweet and beautifully outlined. At times raw emotions
formed their prayers. And God listened, and He answered.

How do we begin praying? The Word of God is an effective
prayer tool. My personal prayer life began with a determined
purpose to know God. How does one approach God? You come
before Him boldly and confidently. If you have sinned, don't run
from Him, but acknowledge your sin: "He is faithful and just to

forgive us our sins and to cleanse us from all unrighteousness" (1 John 1:9).

One time when I was praying for a loved one who I felt was too hardened for God to reach, God said, "If I could convict and convince you of sin, righteousness, and judgment, I know how to reach him." Ouch! The truth hurt, but it led me to repentance. He calls us by His grace, not by our works of righteousness.

> The Lord comes...to convict all who are ungodly among them of all their ungodly deeds which they have committed in an ungodly way.
>
> —JUDE 14–15

Daily Prayer

Father, I come before the throne of grace to receive mercy and find grace to help me in this hour of need. Lord, You are my refuge and my fortress: my God, in You will I trust. You are my goodness and my fortress, my high tower, and my deliverer; my shield, and again I say You are the One in whom I trust. O Lord, my strength, You are my refuge in the day of affliction, anguish, distress, and adversity. If God be for me, who can be against me? In the name of Jesus, I decree that I am strong in the Lord and the power of His might. Amen.

Day 5

Guard Your Thought Patterns

Daily Scripture Verse

Whatever things are true, whatever things are noble, whatever things are just, whatever things are pure,

whatever things are lovely, whatever things are of good report, if there is any virtue and if there is anything praiseworthy—meditate on these things.

—PHILIPPIANS 4:8

*A*s God's Word analyzes our thoughts and the intents of our hearts, selfish, self-centered thought patterns, wrong motives, and ungodly attitudes are exposed. To grow spiritually, we must repent, renew our minds, and submit to the constant ministry of transformation by the Spirit. You have the power of choice, and you have God's ability to bring your thoughts under subjection to the will of God. A clear conscience enables you to come to God with bold confidence. Old thought patterns are exchanged for His thoughts and His motivations.

There are many motivational intentions for intercessory prayer. Sometimes, adverse circumstances call us to prayer. As you pray, your capacity to pray is expanded. While praying in my bedroom one day my spiritual eyes were opened, and I saw a long parade marching before me. The people were dressed in various native costumes, and I realized that I was praying for the nations of the world. God confirmed this from Psalm 2:8. Another time while reading the newspaper, the Spirit prompted me to pray for a popular singing group. Always be alert and persevere in prayer, guarding your thought patterns about the things you are praying for.

Ask of Me, and I will give You
The nations for Your inheritance,
And the ends of the earth for Your possession.

—PSALM 2:8

Daily Prayer

Father, I repent and renounce the sin of criticizing and judging others. In the name of Jesus, I cast down critical,

judgmental, condemning thoughts toward others. I will not judge, criticize, or condemn them. In the name of Jesus, help me get the beam of timber out of my own eye, and then I will see clearly how to take the tiny particle out of my brother's eye. I bind my mind to love, mercy, compassion, and God's grace, in the name of Jesus, the name that is above all names. Amen.

Day 1

The Call to Prayer

Daily Scripture Verse

> Then He spoke a parable to them, that men always ought to pray and not lose heart.
>
> —LUKE 18:1

*T*he time has come for everyone to answer the call to prayer. Prayer will usher the church of Jesus Christ into the unity of the faith under the direction of God-appointed leadership. Scriptural prayers issuing from pure hearts in an atmosphere of harmony and agreement will avail much. God called us to keep the unity of the spirit through the bond of peace. (See Ephesians 4:3.)

Paul prayed diligently and consistently for the churches. His prayers always focused on relationships, spiritual development, and emotional wholeness. Prayer prepared them to receive instructions on how to get along with one another here in this world environment.

Although there are certain "called-out" ones who serve as intercessors in the church, everyone is called to a lifestyle of prayer. In Matthew 21:13 Jesus noted, "It is written, 'My house shall be called a house of prayer.'" Individually, each person is a temple of the Holy Spirit, or a house of prayer. Together, we make up one great household of prayer.

When each one of us assumes our respective position on the prayer team, esteeming one another, miracles take place—the plan of God will unfold—and we become one in Christ Jesus so that the world will know that God the Father has sent His Son for their salvation. In this the Father is glorified!

> You are…members of the household of God, having been built on the foundation of the apostles and

prophets, Jesus Christ Himself being the chief cornerstone, in whom the whole building, being fitted together, grows into a holy temple in the Lord.

—EPHESIANS 2:19–21

Daily Prayer

Hear my prayer, O God; listen to the words of my mouth. The moment I pray, You send an angel for my words, and Your answer is on its way to me. I purpose with the help of the Holy Spirit that I will always have an excellent spirit and remain in right standing with You. May the words of my mouth and the meditation of my heart be pleasing in Your sight, O Lord, my Rock and my Redeemer. In the name of Jesus, I pray. Amen.

Day 2

Purpose to Pray

Daily Scripture Verse

Stand therefore…praying always with all prayer and supplication in the Spirit, being watchful to this end with all perseverance and supplication for all the saints.

—EPHESIANS 6:14, 18

*P*rayer is something that we purpose to do. Personal procrastination leads to prayerlessness, a sin of which we must repent. John Wesley said, "It seems God is limited by our prayer life—that He can do nothing for humanity unless someone asks Him." Unity in the church will become a reality when we assume our joyous responsibility of praying for all saints ev-

erywhere and for the ministers of the gospel according to God's will.

For a pastor or ministry head whose prayer life is slipping away from him, responsibilities can be overwhelming, and personal issues or the needs of others become so mountainous that he feels powerless. But we know the One who is all powerful, and it is imperative that we schedule time to fellowship with the Father in the inner chamber. The Lord is our strength, He is our wisdom, and here in communion with the Holy Spirit we become intimately acquainted with Him.

When prayer seems futile and you don't feel like praying, tell Him. He knows how to help you and how to draw you to His side. No one comes to the place of prayer except the Father draws him. "Draw me nearer, nearer, precious Lord." Don't waste precious time berating yourself for a lack of prayer, but purpose to respond, even if you have to cancel other less important activities. Stir up the gift that is within you by praying!

> Let us draw near with a true heart in full assurance of faith, having our hearts sprinkled from an evil conscience and our bodies washed with pure water.
> —Hebrews 10:22

Daily Prayer

Lord, I seek You with my whole heart and desire to walk in Your ways. I praise You today with uprightness of heart. With my whole heart I seek You; do not let me wander from Your commandments! Your Word I have hidden in my heart that I might not sin against You. Blessed are You, O Lord! Teach me Your statues, in the name of Jesus, I pray. You are a rewarder of those who diligently seek You. Amen.

Day 3

Satan Hates Your Prayers

Daily Scripture Verse

When you pray, go into your room, and when you
have shut your door, pray to your Father who is in the
secret place; and your Father who sees in secret will
reward you openly.

—MATTHEW 6:6

Satan understands the power of prayer, and he plots to prevent us from praying creative, reflective prayers. He works to intensify our unresolved issues such as an inappropriate need to please people. Our need to fix others or a false feeling of responsibility devours our energy, and we have less time to pray.

In *The Screwtape Letters* by C. S. Lewis, Screwtape, an instructor of demons, is training Wormwood, the new recruit, to be an expert tempter. He writes, "You no longer need a good book, which he really likes, to keep him from his prayers or his work or his sleep; a column of advertisements in yesterday's paper will do. You can make him waste his time not only in conversation he enjoys with people whom he likes but also in conversations with those he cares nothing about, on subjects that bore him."[2] Satan fears the consistent, fervent prayers of the righteous.

Purpose to pray; don't give up or lose heart. Begin with a plan, and ask the Holy Spirit to help you develop the process of prayer that will most effectively open your mind to God's presence. Schedule a time to pray. It is good to begin with a psalm of thanksgiving and praise. You may sing a hymn or a spontaneous

song of joy. Pray the Scriptures, and imagine walking or running with Jesus in solitude—along the seashore, beside quiet streams, in a garden of luscious, sweet smelling roses, or on mountain peaks. Talk to God, not in pious, religious words, but in your normal manner of speech as you would talk with your best friend.

God is concerned with everything that concerns you. Pray about the day's activities, and practice God's presence throughout the day. Pray for others knowing that your prayers are reaching out and encircling them. Pray positive prayers according to the will of God. Your words have power. Always submit to God's will in any given situation. Take a few moments to be quiet, listening for God's instructions. Keep a prayer journal, listing those for whom you pray, and record God's personal message to you. Pray with purpose.

> Give to the Lord the glory due His name;
> Bring an offering, and come into His courts.
> Oh, worship the Lord in the beauty of holiness!
> —Psalm 96:8–9

Daily Prayer

Father, in the name of Jesus I commit to pray with purpose, and not give up. This is the confidence that I have in You, that if I ask anything according to Your will, I know that You hear me. Since I know that You hear me, whatsoever I ask, I know that I have the petitions that I desire of You. Father God, You are with me, You are in me, and I thank You for helping me. Amen.

Day 4

Let the Past Go, and Move On

Daily Scripture Verse

> The LORD God is my strength;
> He will make my feet like deer's feet,
> And He will make me walk on my high hills.
>
> —HABAKKUK 3:19

*H*annah Hurnard, the author of many devotional classics, was born in Britain. For many years she lived in Israel where she served as a missionary with the Church's Ministry to the Jews. In her book *Hinds' Feet on High Places* she dramatizes the journey each of us must take before we can live in "high places."[3] In this allegory we can follow a young woman, Much-Afraid, on her spiritual journey through difficult places with her two companions, Sorrow and Suffering.

I have met a few people who believe that sorrow and suffering is the cross they must bear, and they never expect to arrive on the high places. Each loss they suffer, each obstacle in their path is proof that God has placed them on earth to be disappointed. This misbelief robs them of the more abundant life Jesus gives to every believer. The good news is that the love of Christ comes between divine justice and our guilty souls. Jesus bore our sins in His own body on the tree. And as believers you have victory over your spiritual enemies, sin, Satan, and the world. You have the power to let go of past hurts and disappointments. God intends for you to have a happy frame of soul and walk on the high places above your circumstances.

Your heavenly Father knew you before the foundation of the world, and His plans for you include peace and joy. God knows

the future, and His plans for you are good and full of hope. This does not mean that you will be spared pain, suffering, or hardship, but God will see you through to a glorious conclusion. Letting go of the past will help to strengthen your prayer life.

> For I know the thoughts that I think toward you, says the LORD, thoughts of peace and not of evil, to give you a future and a hope.
>
> —JEREMIAH 29:11

Daily Prayer

> *Father, I thank You for delivering me from the power of darkness and translating me into the kingdom of Your dear Son. I resist the temptation to worry, because the law of the Spirit of life in Christ Jesus has made me free from the law of sin and death. I humble myself under Your mighty hand that in due time You may exalt me, casting all my cares—all my anxieties, all my worries, all my concerns—once and for all on You, in the name of Jesus Christ of Nazareth. Amen.*

Day 5

Prayer Goes Before Signs and Wonders

Daily Scripture Verse

> Now, Lord…grant to Your servants that with all boldness they may speak Your word, by stretching out Your hand to heal, and that signs and wonders may be done through the name of Your holy Servant Jesus.
>
> —ACTS 4:29–30

Throughout the Scriptures we see that God performed signs and wonders to get the attention of the people. God called to Moses from a burning bush that didn't burn up. It is written in Acts 7:36, "He brought them out, after he had shown wonders and signs in the land of Egypt, and in the Red Sea, and in the wilderness forty years."

Signs and wonders accompanied the ministry of Jesus. "Men of Israel, hear these words: Jesus of Nazareth, a Man attested by God to you by miracles, wonders, and signs which God did through Him in your midst, as you yourselves also know." (Acts 2:22).

Signs and wonders are evident in the Book of Acts. The primary emphasis in this book is the activity of the Holy Spirit—or the acts of the apostles. Before Jesus ascended into heaven He instructed His disciples that they were to wait in Jerusalem until they were endued with power from on high. In Acts 2, the Holy Spirit swept in on them like a rushing wind, and they were enabled to speak the wonderful gospel of Jesus Christ in all the languages of the Mediterranean world. The Holy Spirit fell upon the Gentiles while Peter was preaching. The Spirit caught up Philip and took him into the desert region to witness to the Ethiopian eunuch. The Spirit directed the church in Antioch to set apart Saul and Barnabas as missionaries. In Acts 2:43 we read, "Everyone was filled with awe, and many wonders and miraculous signs were done by the apostles" (NIV).

Are we willing to pay the price to experience these signs and wonders? What is the price? Acts 2:41–42 gives us the secret, the price that we have to pay.

> Those *who accepted his message* were baptized, and about three thousand were added to their number that day. They *devoted themselves* to the apostles' teaching

and to the fellowship, *to the breaking of bread and to prayer.*

Daily Prayer

Lord, I acknowledge You as my strength, my rock, my fortress, my deliverer, and my shield. Even though enemies rise up against me, they will not triumph over me. I choose to walk in a manner that is pleasing to You, and You make my enemies to be at peace with me. You cause them to flee from me seven ways. How grateful I am that You, my Lord, would honor me by preparing a table of abundance for me in the presence of my enemies. In Jesus' name, amen.

Day 1

God Hears the Cries of His People

Daily Scripture Verse

> Hear a just cause, O LORD,
> Attend to my cry;
> Give ear to my prayer which is not from deceitful lips.
> —PSALM 17:1

*P*rayer originated in the heart of God, our Father. God, the Holy Spirit, hovers over the church, awaiting prayers that are prayed according to God's Word, who became flesh and dwelt among us. Just as in days gone by so shall it be again. God's people pray, He hears their prayers, and events occur according to His plan.

Jesus spoke about the interaction of the Holy Spirit and the praying church: "Rivers of living water will flow out from within" (John 7:38, NLT). This living water will go forth into the desert places repairing the waste places, reviving ancient ruins that have lain there many generations. The living water is for the healing of the nations (Rev. 22:2). Did God not say: "Ask of Me, and I will give You the nations for Your inheritance, and the ends of the earth for Your possession" (Ps. 2:8)?

In these last days a multitude of God's people who are called to be watchmen on the wall are observing the signs, and prayer is uttered according to His Word. The prayers that go forth are powerful scriptural prayers filling the heavens, preparing the way for the manifestation of the sons of God, and every knee shall bow and every tongue confess that Jesus Christ is Lord.

God is watching over His Word to perform it. The church is His voice in the earth, and when we pray in agreement with the Father, the Son, and the Holy Spirit, we can be confident of this very thing:

So shall My word be that goes forth out of My mouth: it shall not return to Me void [without producing any effect, useless], but it shall accomplish that which I please and purpose, and it shall prosper in the thing for which I sent it.

—Isaiah 55:11, amp

Daily Prayer

Father, by the grace You have given me, I trust You and Your promises. You said that You would never leave me nor forsake me. You are always with me, in every personal and business situation. Thank You for the Holy Spirit, who is my comforter, counselor, helper, advocate, intercessor, strengthener, teacher, and guide. Though fear arises, I will not be dismayed, because You uphold me with Your victorious right hand in Jesus' name. You are my helper. Amen.

Day 2

Pray for the People

Daily Scripture Verse

I thank my God upon every remembrance of you, always in every prayer of mine making request for you all with joy...being confident of this very thing, that He who has begun a good work in you will complete it until the day of Jesus Christ.

—Philippians 1:3–4, 6

As the body of Christ we are interdependent, and it is our responsibility to pray for one another that we may all be healed and restored to a spiritual tone of mind and heart. Each

person is precious and is given special assignments from God. Everyone is called to different areas of prayer, and together we fulfill and enforce the triumphant victory of Jesus Christ. You are not alone. There is always a remnant of people praying with you for the will of God to be manifested on earth.

Over the years I have learned to give attention to feelings of dissatisfaction. My first encounter with signs of spiritual growth occurred just as winter was giving way to spring. I felt restless and asked, "Father, what is wrong with me?" God was leading me into another level of prayer. He was calling me to pray for others. The names and faces of people were creeping in and distracting me from my prayer focus. It seemed that all my needs were met, and I simply wanted to become more intimately acquainted with Him. I thought that my mind was wandering away from the presence of God, and I felt distraught. The names and faces wouldn't go away. Little did I realize that God was preparing me for an event that would challenge me to learn to pray prayers of intercession.

To reclaim my position of praise and worship in the throne room, I began to pray for people. Not knowing their situations, I would pray the prayers of Paul from Ephesians, Philippians, and Colossians. To my amazement I would hear from someone I had prayed for, or actually meet someone at the mall or at the grocery store—people who I had not heard from or seen in years. The Holy Spirit used these encounters to teach me that the "distractions" during my prayer time were nudges to pray for others. Praise and worship opened the door for these prayer assignments.

There were times I felt overwhelmed. How could I possibly have time to study, fellowship with God, and pray for my family members and all these others as well? Turning to the Psalms I would read aloud from Psalms 1, 8, 27, 100, 103, and

many others. God never failed to renew my strength and to give me His prayer objectives. The Holy Spirit always knows where prayer is most needed at a given time.

> And this I pray, that your love may abound still more and more in knowledge and all discernment, that you may approve the things that are excellent, that you may be sincere and without offense till the day of Christ.
>
> —Philippians 1:9–10

Daily Prayer

> *Father, I thank You for my friends. You have filled our mouths with kindness, and we speak words of grace into each other's lives. We are there to laugh and cry together; we trust each other, encouraging one another in the Lord. We confess our faults to one another and pray for one another that we may be healed and restored to a spiritual tone of mind and heart. Thank You, Jesus, for teaching me how to be a good friend. Amen.*

Day 3

Continue Praying

Daily Scripture Verse

> For the weapons of our warfare are not carnal but mighty in God for pulling down strongholds, casting down arguments and every high thing that exalts itself against the knowledge of God, bringing every thought into captivity to the obedience of Christ.
>
> —2 Corinthians 10:4–5

Sometimes I would react emotionally to spiritual revelation and momentarily abort my prayers. God is faithful, and if you continue praying, He will teach and train you in the law of the Spirit of life in Christ Jesus. You will cry, you will feel emotionally distraught at times, but you will learn to be led by the Spirit rather than your emotions.

God created you to participate in His purposes. You are called to be an agent of Jesus Christ by the will of God. As His agent of prayer you are to hold the thoughts, feelings, and purposes of His heart. The mind of Christ has to develop within you so that you can cast down personal imaginations and religious dogmas that set themselves up against the knowledge of God. To proclaim the will of God, you have to know the will of God.

The Prayers That Avail Much˙ family books are a revelation of the steps that led me to where I am today. I began to write out my prayers, and as I prayed them, the Holy Spirit wrote them on my mind and the tablets of my heart. As you pray the will of God, your faith that begins as a grain of mustard seed develops and grows. Even the least amount of faith contains the power to remove mountains.

Remain in the school of prayer. Purpose to know God; make a commitment to read, study, and meditate on His Word. Commit to pray, and don't give up. Make an appointment with God, and keep your appointment. Acknowledge the Holy Spirit. He takes the things of Jesus and reveals them unto you, and you become a channel of prayer for all nations. To know Jesus is to know the Father. Pray without ceasing.

> But you, beloved, building yourselves up on your most
> holy faith, praying in the Holy Spirit, keep yourselves
> in the love of God, looking for the mercy of our Lord
> Jesus Christ unto eternal life.
>
> —JUDE 20–21

> *Lord, You are my rock, my fortress, my deliverer, my God, my strength, in whom I will trust, my buckler, and the horn of my salvation. You are my high tower. For Your name's sake lead me and guide me. You brought me up out of a horrible pit, out of the miry clay, and set my feet upon a rock, and You established my goings. You are my strong habitation, whereunto I may continually resort. You gave the commandment to save me, for You are my rock and my fortress. In the name of Jesus, You are my foundation. Amen.*

Day 4

Praying for Adult Children

Daily Scripture Verse

> Satan has asked for you, that he may sift you as wheat. But I have prayed for you, that your faith should not fail; and when you have returned to Me, strengthen your brethren.
>
> —LUKE 22:31–32

Several years ago I talked with the leader of a Christian rehabilitation ministry, and he said that the most difficult young people to help are those of Christian parents. He went on to say, "They refuse to let their children suffer the consequences of their behavior. Often, they are concerned about how they will look in the eyes of others, or fear being judged and found lacking. Some will question their faith."

When we see our adult children under attack we immediately begin "fighting" the devil. Satan becomes the focus of our

prayers, and we fail to realize that each individual has to walk his own spiritual journey by his own free will. If he is to mature and develop character, we can't walk his path for him. We have to allow each child to develop character and wait on God to direct our prayers.

In Luke 22:31–32 we read a conversation Jesus had with Peter, which shows the foreknowledge Jesus had of the trial Simon was facing. Even though Jesus knew Satan's plan for Simon, He did not rebuke the devil; He didn't stop the attack. He did not try to control Peter's decision. Instead He prayed for Simon Peter, and He prayed for the positive results of Peter's outcome.

We know that Peter yielded to temptation, but we only have to read the Book of Acts and Peter's epistles to understand that God's will was done in his life. God turned what Satan meant for destruction into development of Peter's character. Peter fulfilled his divine destiny.

We must trust God with our adult children—even when we can see the spiritual trials they are facing and the plan of Satan to ensnare them. We are so quick to blame the devil and to attack him with a vengeance. Where is our trust? "Lord," we pray, "You have the power to deliver my child from the attack of the enemy. Don't let Satan harass him." Jesus, however, keeps praying, "Father, don't let his faith fail, but use this time to purify his faith." Do we want it our way or God's way? Remember, you were not too hard for God, and neither is the adult child for whom you are praying.

> We…do not cease to pray for you, and to ask that you
> may be filled with the knowledge of His will in all wis-
> dom and spiritual understanding; that you may have a
> walk worthy of the Lord, fully pleasing Him.
> —Colossians 1:9–10

> *Thank You, Father, that our children belong to You, and*
> *we are heirs together with Christ. We thank You, Father*
> *God, that our family will set forth the wonderful deeds and*
> *display the virtues and perfections of Him who called us*
> *out of darkness into His marvelous light, in the name of*
> *Jesus I pray. We rejoice because our children are walking*
> *in truth. Amen.*

Day 5

When We Don't Know How to Pray

Daily Scripture Verse

> The Spirit also helps in our weaknesses. For we do not
> know what we should pray for as we ought, but the
> Spirit Himself makes intercession for us with groan-
> ings which cannot be uttered.
>
> —ROMANS 8:26

When we need to know how to pray prayers that avail much, the Holy Spirit is faithful to help us apply God's Word to all of our situations. When we look to Him, the Holy Spirit will direct our prayers.

My dad, Buck Griffin, was diagnosed with dementia in 1996. From the onset of his dementia, we prayed and inter-ceded to God for his healing. But when we saw no improvement, I became discouraged. I didn't understand why God didn't answer our prayers for my father. He had served God all his life; people had been raised from death beds, fully recovered when he prayed the simple prayer of faith. Now he could no longer

even read the Bible. Before I realized it, I had opened the door to hurt, disappointment, and anger.

The Holy Spirit led me to read Romans 8:26–27 in my Women of Destiny Bible. Noticing that Paula Sandford had written a letter referring to this verse, I read how this passage of Scripture had comforted her after her dad developed Alzheimer's disease. "We serve a Lord who understands us completely and compassionately...who intercedes for us according to the perfect will of God." When we do not know how we ought to pray, the Spirit Himself intercedes for us.

My prayers for my dad changed. "Father, I lean not unto my own understanding, but in my role as caregiver I acknowledge You and trust You. Holy Spirit, I ask You to direct my prayers for my dad, Buck Griffin. Give his caregivers wisdom to care for him, and show me how to communicate with him. You love him more than I do. He has said that he will live until Jesus comes. Have mercy on him; either heal him completely, or come and receive him unto Yourself. His times are in Your hands." My brother and sister were in agreement.

In those last few days before God released his spirit from his deteriorating mind and body, he recognized family members again. He never lost his dry sense of humor, and he never ceased to be appreciative and kind to others. His life was his testimony, and his ministry continues in the lives of ministers who are actively serving as pastors, teachers, apostles, prophets, and evangelists today. Dementia could not silence the Word, which lived big in A. H. "Buck" Griffin.

In situations where you don't know how to pray, acknowledge God and submit to the leadership of the Holy Spirit. He searches the hearts of everyone concerned, and He knows the mind of the Spirit. After you have prayed, rest assured of this:[4]

We are assured and know that [God being a partner in their labor] all things work together and are [fitting into a plan] for good to and for those who love God and are called according to [His] design and purpose.

—ROMANS 8:28, AMP

Daily Prayer

Father, I thank You for all the pioneers who blazed the way, all the veterans cheering me on. I will never quit! I lay aside every weight and every sin that would hinder me. I fix my eyes on Jesus, the author and perfecter of my faith, who for the joy set before Him endured the cross, scorning its shame, and sat down at the right hand of the throne of God. I am running to win. I press toward the goal for the prize of the upward call of God in Christ Jesus. Amen.

Day 1

When God's People Pray

Daily Scripture Verse

Enlarge the place of your tent…
Lengthen your cords,
And strengthen your stakes.…
For you shall expand to the right and to the left,
And your descendants will inherit the nations,
And make the desolate cities inhabited.

—ISAIAH 54:2–3

*A*s a stay-at-home mom, Rose's world was very small. In fact, some days she wondered if her children would ever grow up, or would she forever be "Mommy"? Then Jesus reached way down for her; He came to her world, and she was never the same. She began a new walk, and prayer became a normal part of her day.

Every day is an adventure in the Spirit, and God will expand your vision of the world. On that day many years ago, Rose began a new adventure in prayer. Her three older children were in school, and the baby was asleep. As was her custom she went into her bedroom where she knelt to pray. The sun shining through the window welcomed her, and she was transported into the Sonlight of God's love. Kneeling there, enjoying the warmth and the presence of her Lord, she became aware of other people. God opened her eyes, and she saw a parade of people dressed in native costumes walking before her. Overwhelmed, she asked, "Lord, what does this mean?"

God expanded her vision beyond the four walls of her home. That day she caught a glimpse of the heart of God and praised Him for including her in His plan for man. God loves

the whole world. Jesus died that men and women of every nation and tribe might be free. Walking in the love of God became her great quest, her aim in life.

God will enlarge our capacity to love that we might understand His heart and see as He sees. He has involved His church in His plan. Our prayers prepare the way for His will to be done on earth even as it is in heaven. Let us be about our Father's business.

> We also pray always for you that our God would count you worthy of this calling, and fulfill all the good pleasure of His goodness and the work of faith with power.
> —2 THESSALONIANS 1:11

Daily Prayer

> *We decree on the authority of Your Word that this gospel of the kingdom will be preached in the entire world as a witness to all the nations, and then the end will come (Matt. 24:14). Lord of the harvest, we pray that You will send laborers into the fields that are white unto harvest. When God's people pray, You work to fulfill Your will on earth, as it is in heaven.*

Day 2

Teaching Your Children to Pray

Daily Scripture Verse

> As He was praying in a certain place…one of His disciples said to Him, "Lord, teach us to pray."
> —LUKE 11:1

*O*nly a few short years ago we sent our children off to public school with confidence knowing that they were in a

safe place. Tragically, this has changed, and increasingly parents are turning to prayer. It is our responsibility to teach our children that God will hear them when they pray whether at home, church, school, or on the playground. Hasty or superficial prayers will not teach or train them to pray with confidence. Prayer is developed by precept and practice.

Communication with God is available to everyone at all times. We can pray aloud, or we can pray silently. Verbal prayer may have been taken out of our schools, but we can give our children hope by assuring them that our heavenly Father hears silent prayers. He knows our thoughts from afar, even before we think them. One of the keys for an effective prayer life is practicing the presence of Jesus—aware that He is always ready to hear us when we pray.

Why should we practice prayer and teach our children to pray? Jesus, who is our example, prayed to the Father, and He instructed us to pray and not give up or lose heart. We can either pray our own thoughts, or we can return His Word to Him through prayer. The Bible tells us that His Word will not return to Him without producing results.

Take time to pray meaningful, creative prayers with your children. The Bible is God speaking to you, and as you pray scriptural prayers with them each morning and evening, they will learn the value of prayer. The power of God will protect them; the presence of God will go with them.

> The angel of the LORD encamps all around those who
>   fear Him,
> And delivers them.
>
> —PSALM 34:7

Daily Prayer

Father, in the name of Jesus, we thank You for Your angels that You have assigned to our children. You have given

Your angels charge over them, to keep them in all their ways. We reverence You and acknowledge You as our Lord and Savior. Thank You for the angel of the Lord who encamps all around our children and delivers them from perilous situations. We bless our children that they may be powerful in the land and fulfill their divine destiny. Amen.

Day 3

United in Prayer We Stand

Daily Scripture Verse

I have declared to them Your name, and will declare it, that the love with which You loved Me may be in them, and I in them.

—John 17:26

There was a strange calmness as Jesus' disciples went about their designated assignments for the Feast of the Passover. They did not know that the time had come for Jesus to leave this world, and that it would be their last supper with Him.

Jesus had given His disciples specific instructions, and each one secretly wondered why this Passover was different. Even in their perplexity, they felt honored that Jesus desired to eat the Passover in a secluded room with just them. Everything was in order as they sat down at the table. While the disciples were eating and talking among themselves in low tones, Jesus took a piece of unleavened bread in His strong, brown hands and blessed it. Breaking it, He said, "Take, eat; this is My body."

Then Jesus blessed the cup saying, "Drink all of it; for this is My blood of the covenant, which is shed for many unto remission of sins. Do this in remembrance of Me."

When we eat the bread and drink from the cup, we become one with Christ. This union prepares us to live in a community of mutual love, service, and humility. Jesus talked to His disciples revealing spiritual truths and explaining His relationship with the Father. He promised to send the Holy Spirit to be our teacher and comforter. He will lead us into all reality. Jesus is in the Father, we are in Him, and He is in us. We are one.

The disciples listened intently as Jesus taught them about their vital union with Him. He identified the Father as the Vine-dresser, Himself as the vine, and His followers as the branches. Grafted into the one true vine, we are connected—unified in Him. As He talked with them about the future He said, "I will no longer speak to you in parables, but tell you plainly about the Father. You will make your requests to Him in My name." We are one, and united in prayer we stand.

The trumpet call has gone forth—it is time to unite with Jesus in His prayer that we will be one even as He and the Father are one. It is time to tear down "strongholds" that have separated us. A new day is dawning; never has there been such a time as this. United in prayer we stand.

> The glory which You gave Me I have given them, that they may be one just as We are one: I in them, and You in Me; that they may be made perfect in one.
>
> —John 17:22–23

Daily Prayer

> Heavenly Father, You made me what I am and gave me a new life; long ages ago You planned that I should spend my life in helping others. You are a great God, a loving God, a giving God, and I purpose to imitate You. The end of all things is at hand, and I will be serious and watchful in my prayers. Above all things, and by Your grace, I give

myself to a fervent love for others—a love that covers a multitude of sins, in the name of Jesus. Amen.

Day 4

The Prayer of Agreement

Daily Scripture Verse

> Again I tell you, if two of you on earth agree (harmonize together, make a symphony together) about whatever [anything and everything] they may ask, it will come to pass and be done for them by My Father in heaven.
>
> —Matthew 18:19, amp

Learning to live in harmony with other members of the body of Christ can be an awesome responsibility. We bring our hang-ups, our unresolved issues, emotional wounds, and unacknowledged anger to the table. God's intention is for us to mature, to receive healing for our emotional wounds, to resolve issues according to the Word of God, and to forgive one another. He expects us to get rid of our hang-ups and love one another.

Learning to walk in love is probably the cross that we all bear. But the dividends are too wonderful to ignore. By seeking first the kingdom of God and His righteousness (His way of doing and being right), we order our steps in His Word. Living in harmony requires us to encourage one another and pray for one another that we may all be healed and restored to a spiritual tone of mind and heart (James 5:16). Praying scriptural prayers has brought me into a more intimate relationship with our Father. Freely I receive; freely I give prayer support speaking words of grace to everyone who listens.

We live in harmony with one another so that prayers will be effective as we pray for all men everywhere, for governments families, the body of Christ; for ministers, for the unity of the body of Christ. When the world sees the body of Christ united, walking in love with one another, they will know that God the Father loves them as much as He loves His Son who came to take away the sins of the world and destroy the works of the devil.

The Holy Spirit teaches us to pray all manner of prayer, including the prayer of agreement. The prayer of agreement dispels the darkness, preparing the way for the End-Time harvest. Jesus is coming again!

> I…beseech you to walk worthy of the calling with which you were called, with all lowliness and gentleness, with longsuffering, bearing with one another in love, endeavoring to keep the unity of the Spirit in the bond of peace.
>
> —EPHESIANS 4:1–3

Daily Prayer

> *Father, we thank You for saving us from wrath through Christ. If when we were enemies we were reconciled to You through the death of Your Son, much more, having been reconciled, we shall be saved by His life. We also rejoice in You through our Lord Jesus Christ, through whom we have now received reconciliation. We shall rejoice in You and be glad in the name of Jesus. Amen.*

Day 5

Meeting the Lord

Daily Scripture Verse

> The Lord…drew me out of many waters.
> He delivered me from my strong enemy….
> He also brought me out into a broad place;
> He delivered me because He delighted in me.
> —2 SAMUEL 22:14, 17–18, 20

The teenager had always been drawn to the Bible that lay on a table in their home, but after trying to read the first words of the New Testament she closed it and walked away. Once again, the voice interrupted her musings, "When will you get right with God?" Once again she answered, "When I meet Him for myself, and I will before I die." This conversation took place in the recesses of Donnis's mind for as far back as she could remember.

Her family attended church once a month when the circuit preacher came to their farming community. At the close of each service he said, "The doors of the church are open. If anyone wants to become a Christian, walk down this aisle and join the church." She wasn't interested in joining the church; she wanted to meet God.

When Donnis was fifteen, her family heard about a revival that was being held at another church, and her dad was warned by neighbors to stay away from those holy-rollers. All the talk about "those folks" aroused a desire in Mr. Brock to go check things out. One night after coming in from the fields, he loaded up his family, and off they went. Sitting in the last pew between her two brothers, Donnis loved the lively music, but she ound it difficult to follow the thunderous sermon.

At last the congregation stood, and the minister said, "If anyone wants to meet God, come down to the altar." Donnis ran down to the front. Kneeling she lifted her eyes to the ceiling, and to her delight the roof rolled back and a light of pure joy descended and rested upon her. On the way back to the farm no one spoke, but Donnis wasn't dismayed. She was overflowing with the joy of meeting the Lord.

Arriving home, Papa and the boys attended to the horses and put away the wagon before coming inside; everyone was silent until Mama broke the holy hush saying, "Let's go to bed."

"Mama," Donnis declared, "we have to pray before we go to bed." Everyone stood and listened as Donnis prayed the first prayer ever prayed in their home. Later, all her family was born again and filled with the Spirit of the living God. The salvation of a young girl prepared the way for future generations of gifted ministers.

No one can come to Me unless the Father who sent Me draws him; and I will raise him up at the last day.

—JOHN 6:44

Daily Prayer

Father, I thank You for giving Your only Son that I might be saved. You paid the awesome price of the blood of Your Son to redeem my life from destruction. You looked through the eons of time and chose me as Your very own. The blood of Jesus paid the price for the divine destiny You placed in me, which I purpose to live to the full. Thank You for Your unconditional love and Your ability to love others even as You have loved me. In Jesus' name, I pray. Amen.

Day 1

The *Ifs* of Answered Prayer

Daily Scripture Verse

> Therefore I say to you, whatever things you ask when
> you pray, believe that you receive them, and you will
> have them.
>
> —MARK 11:24

*W*hen circumstances crowd you and pressures crash
down upon you, it is an opportunity to exercise faith,
and trust God to bring about transformation in you, in your
attitudes, and in your motives. God has told us that if we will
pray, we can have our prayers answered. However, He gave one
very important qualification to this promise—He said that we
must believe that we will have our prayers answered. In His
Word, Jesus revealed the all-inclusive conditions of answered
prayer, and He made no allowances for unanswered prayer.

Remember these three important *ifs* to our prayer
requests:

- You can pray for anything, and *if* you believe, you
  have it (Mark 11:24–25).

- *If* you have faith as small as a mustard seed, you
  can say to this mountain, "'Move from here to
  there' and it will move; and nothing will be impossible for you" (Matt. 16:20).

- "*If* you abide in Me, and My words abide in you,
  you will ask what you desire, and it shall be done
  for you" (John 15:7).

Therefore it is of faith that it might be according to
grace, so that the promise might be sure to all the seed,

not only to those who are of the law, but also to those who are of the faith of Abraham...who, contrary to hope, in hope believed.

—ROMANS 4:16, 18

Daily Prayer

Heavenly Father, I purpose to meditate on Your Word day and night. By the grace of God I will be an obedient doer of Your Word, so my pathway will be prosperous and successful. I renew my mind to Your Word, and pray that Your Word will dominate my thoughts, words, and actions. I submit to truth so that I will not be seduced or deceived by the works of the devil. I am strong in You, Lord, and in the power of Your might. In Jesus' name, I pray. Amen.

Day 2

Ask According to God's Will

Daily Scripture Verse

And this is the confidence that we have in him, that, if we ask any thing according to his will, he heareth us.

—1 JOHN 5:14, KJV

Do you know the mind of God concerning the person for whom you are praying? Do you help God out by determining the journey of another person? It is imperative that we abide united with Jesus in His intercession when we intercede.

Oswald Chambers wrote, "It is impossible for us to have living and vital intercession unless we are perfectly and completely sure of God. The greatest destroyer of that confident relationship to God, so necessary for intercession, is our own

personal sympathy and preconceived bias. It is sympathy with ourselves or with others that makes us say, 'I will not allow that thing to happen.' And instantly we are out of that vital connection with God."[5]

It isn't the asking that is difficult—but the waiting. So do not throw away your confidence; it will be richly rewarded. You need to persevere so that when you have done the will of God, you will receive what He has promised. Meet the conditions—God answers prayer!

> Therefore do not cast away your confidence, which has great reward. For you have need of endurance, so that after you have done the will of God, you may receive the promise.
>
> —HEBREWS 10:35–36

Daily Prayer

> *Father, it is true, I can't do a solitary thing on my own: I listen, and then I decide. I'm not out to get my own way but only to carry out Your orders. Not because I think I can do anything of lasting value by myself. My only power and success come from God. Your grace is sufficient for me, for Your power is made perfect in weakness. I can do all things through Christ who strengthens me. Amen.*

Day 3

Trust Him With Your Crisis

Daily Scripture Verse

> Trust in the LORD with all your heart,
> And lean not on your own understanding;
> In all your ways acknowledge Him,

And He shall direct your paths.

PROVERBS 3:5–6

*I*t was in the 1970s that a crisis walked through the front door of our home. Our lives would never be the same. During the years just prior to this situation, I had been developing a personal relationship with God my Father. He loved me, and I loved Him. I knew that I could trust Him with our oldest child, who had become a stranger to us.

Regardless of Satan's strategies to destroy our son, David, over the next thirty years, our God proved again and again that His Word was His will for David. I searched the Scriptures and wrote many prayers. When I was tempted to doubt, I would pray the prayers aloud, knowing that God would always watch over His Word to perform it. I'm not sure when I entered into a lasting agreement with the Father—but a day came when I knew beyond any doubt that Jesus had defeated Satan. I knew that David would be delivered out of the strange land of addictions and would walk in paths of righteousness.

Praise God! He is a God of new beginnings. Today, David is prayer coordinator for Word Ministries located in Roswell, Georgia. His testimony is now on video, "Deliverance From Addictions," and audiotape, "Abiding in God's Love."[6] Trust God with the crises that walk into your home—He will never fail you.

> But I am like a green olive tree in the house of God;
> I trust in the mercy of God forever and ever.
> I will praise You forever,
> Because You have done it.

—PSALM 52:8–9

> *As the deer pants for water, so I long for You, O God. I thirst for You, the living God. In the name of Jesus, I resist discouragement because I expect You to act! For I know that I shall again have plenty of reason to praise You for all that You will do. You are my help! You are my God! I place my trust in You, and I shall again praise You for Your wondrous help; You make me smile again, for You are my God. Amen.*

Day 4

Commit to Pray, and Never Give Up

Daily Scripture Verse

> The first thing I want you to do is pray. Pray every way you know how, for everyone you know.
> —1 TIMOTHY 2:1, THE MESSAGE

Do not give up! Now is the time to pray! The spiritual walls of our nation are in disrepair. The situation may look overwhelming, but we serve a mighty God.

Never stop praying! The Holy Spirit, who is an intercessor who cannot fail, comes alongside and helps you when you don't know how to pray. Prayer opens the door to a more intimate relationship with God, which places you in a position to pray in agreement with His will.

In Ezekiel 22:30, we see that God is calling for intercessors who will stand in the gap before Him on behalf of the land. These intercessors become a wall of faithful people united in their efforts to resist evil.

Standing in the gap is made effective by many spiritual

tools one of the most powerful is praise. What is praise? Praise eulogizes God, conveying the idea of boastful singing or speaking about His glorious virtues and honor. Blessed be the God and Father of our Lord Jesus Christ! Speak well of our Father, tell of His goodness, adore Him and give Him an audible celebration. Praise might be quiet and contemplative. Whether your praise is boisterous or quiet, it will still and silence the enemy (Ps. 8:2; 9:6). God inhabits the prayers of His people, and His manifested presence frustrates the tactics of the enemy.

Standing in the gap with joyful praise opens prison doors, preparing the way of salvation (Acts 16:25–26). Praise releases the power to overthrow satanic captivity! Praise repels and replaces the spirit of heaviness, releases the power and the anointing that destroys yokes and moves burdens. Praise will birth victory in the face of warfare. Praise stops the advancement of wickedness and drives out the temptations to sin (Ps. 7:14–17).

Offer your prayers of praise to God for all seasons. Bless the Lord at all times; let His praises be continually in your mouth! During this time of turmoil and unrest let us stand shoulder to shoulder in orderly array against the forces of darkness, standing in the gap with praise!

I encourage you to reaffirm your commitment to pray and never turn coward, faint, lose heart, or give up. United in prayer we are making a difference—praying prayers that avail much for all nations.

> Son of man, I have made you a watchman for the house of Israel; therefore hear a word from My mouth, and give them warning from Me.
>
> —EZEKIEL 3:17

> *Father, I commit to pray and not give up, standing in the gap before You for my family members and for others who have not yet called upon Your name, asking You to draw them with cords of love. It is Your will that all men should be saved. With the Holy Spirit as my helper, I will blow a trumpet in Zion (our churches) and sound the alarm, warning all who live in the land that the day of the Lord is coming. It is close at hand. Amen.*

Day 5

Offer Restoration and Unity

Daily Scripture Verse

> For these things I weep;
> My eye, my eye overflows with water;
> Because the comforter, who should restore my life,
> Is far from me.

—Lamentations 1:16

Prayer is one of the pillars of the universal church. Earnest, heartfelt prayer will produce results and bring restoration to wounded intercessors. God has given to us the ministry of reconciliation. God wants His wounded ones restored. We cannot fix one another, but prayer prepares the way for God to undo our erroneous efforts to keep everything together.

Prayer and sound teaching prepare hearts to receive revelations that displace wrong mind-sets, attitudes, and motives. Prayers of manipulation are replaced with Spirit-led prayer. Accusations no longer fly back and forth like a badminton game.

Emotional wounds are healed, and old emotional and psychological patterns of self-protection are brought down.

In prayer, strongholds that emotionally isolate us are destroyed, and we learn to trust one another. An overloaded pastor welcomes a willing heart that commits to pray and lead others in prayer. May we who intercede honor those who brought us the Word of God and imitate their example, following them as they follow God.

If we are to develop healthy relationships within our church families we have to hold the same vision, be of one mind, and be in one accord. In God's presence we learn to esteem others, and our respect for ourselves will be reflected in our respect for others. Then we will have wonderful fellowship and joy with each other, and the blood of Jesus His Son cleanses us from every sin (1 John 1:9).

As a family we acknowledge our flaws, our shortcomings making ourselves accountable—*and pray for one another that we may all be restored to a spiritual tone of mind and heart.* (See James 5:16, AMP.) If you want to see your prayers answered, pray—*and work*—for the restoration and unity of all believers, especially those in your local congregation.

> Confess your trespasses to one another, and pray for one another, that you may be healed. The effective, fervent prayer of a righteous man avails much.
>
> —JAMES 5:16

Daily Prayer

> *Father, in Jesus' name, You are the great reconciler! Of marriages! Of children! Of families! Of brothers and sisters! Of all relationships! It is in Your strength and by Your grace that I will go to the person with whom I have had conflict. You have planted the seed of love in*

my heart, and I will humble myself by asking forgiveness regardless of who was at fault. I pray that the relationship will be healed and the breach mended. I purpose to do this in obedience to Your Word and for Your glory, Lord Jesus. The repairer of breaches in relationships is working on my behalf! Amen.

Day 1

When Your Prayer Center Is Shut Down

Daily Scripture Verse

> Yes, I have loved you with an everlasting love;
> Therefore with lovingkindness I have drawn you.
> Again I will build you, and you shall be rebuilt...
> And shall go forth in the dances of those who rejoice.
> —JEREMIAH 31:3–4

*H*elp! My prayer equipment and recorder needs new batteries. I'm certainly not too busy to pray, but I'm stuck—caught in a fog of inertia. Then I remember that God accepts me where I am. He loves me with an unconditional love, an extravagant love. Will I simply receive the love of a God who is love? By faith, I lay aside the kingdom of self—self-defeat, self-hatred, self-rejection, and self-doubt. Feelings are overwhelming, and I'm struggling to overcome a mental block that doesn't want to come down.

Much to my chagrin my rejoicing device seems to be out of order, and I wonder where the anointing oil might be hiding. My overworked formulas aren't functioning. I feel like throwing in the towel, but I'm not a quitter. That old adage comes back to me, "Winners never quit, and quitters never win." Jesus won a victory for me, and I will not throw away what He has so freely given. By faith, I declare and decree that I am an overcomer by my testimony and the blood of the Lamb.

Yet, the spirit lies dormant, and I don't feel any different. Don't you hate being at a complete loss—not even knowing the questions to ask? The day is marching on, and time is "a' wastin'" can't get anything going, much less anything finished. Sitting at

the computer, staring at the blank screen doesn't spark even a little fire. Where is the Word that has been like fire shut up in my bones? The Bible and the prayer book are open, and I can't concentrate on the words long enough to understand what I am reading. I even know whom to pray for, but everything seems to be by rote and not by the Spirit.

"God, where are You? Why are the heavens shut up?"

Our personal prayer times go through changes with the passages of life, and if we feel powerless, it is time to reopen our prayer center with the keys of gratitude and praise. With each new season comes an opportunity to know another facet of God and to know Him more intimately.

In this private prayer center I find the grace to reevaluate my priorities, and the Holy Spirit helps me make necessary changes that are according to the will of God. My times are in His hands.

> Be of good courage,
> And He shall strengthen your heart,
> All you who hope in the LORD.
>
> —PSALM 31:24

Daily Prayer

Christ is faithful as a Son over God's house. I am His house, if I hold on to my courage and the hope of which I boast. I eagerly expect and hope that I will in no way be ashamed, but will have sufficient courage so that now as always Christ will be exalted in my body, whether by life or by death. Thank You, Holy Spirit, for helping me to stay on my guard and stand firm in the faith. I am a man/woman of courage; strong in the Lord and the power of His might. I will be patient, and take courage, for the coming of the Lord is near. Amen.

Day 2

Too Busy to Pray

Daily Scripture Verse

> But those who wait on the LORD
> Shall renew their strength;
> They shall mount up with wings like eagles,
> They shall run and not be weary,
> They shall walk and not faint.
>
> —ISAIAH 40:31

John Wesley said, "It seems God is limited by our prayer life—that He can do nothing for humanity unless someone asks Him."

Jesus was a man of prayer. Most often He prayed alone, and the supernatural pervaded the natural. The heavens opened, and the will of God was revealed as the natural was changed into the supernatural, and the Father was glorified.

Obviously, the disciples recognized the importance of prayer. And they must have marveled at His ability to minister to the needs of people they knew and lived with. Their lives were transformed. They never dreamed they would leave their life-long occupations to follow a man from village to village.

They knew about miracles, and maybe they thought the day of miracles was over. Their heroes of faith—Moses, Elijah, Elisha, Daniel, and David—accomplished great feats. They knew about supernatural provision, the dead being raised, and lepers healed. The Old Testament prophets performed the miracles Jesus was performing. They asked the Master to teach them to pray!

So often our prayer life is directed by circumstances, and we fail to see the core issues. The Holy Spirit helps us pray when

we don't know how—if we will wait before the Lord in quiet meditation. He will show us things to come. If we ask and listen expectantly, He will give us the wisdom to handle situations correctly. When we've made mistakes, He will give us the tools for setting things right.

Do not allow the enemy to steal your prayer time. If you have been too busy to pray, don't waste time berating yourself. Repent for your prayerlessness, receive your forgiveness, and worship the Father. If you simply don't want to pray, tell Him how you feel, and ask Him to draw you to a place of prayer. Prayer is talking with the Father.

Unite with thousands who are praying for the will of God to be done on earth as it is in heaven. Change begins with us. Our families, our communities, and the nations will acknowledge that Jesus is Lord! Purpose to pray prayers that avail much!

> As the deer pants for the water brooks,
> So pants my soul for You, O God.
> My soul thirsts for God, for the living God.
> When shall I come and appear before God?
> —PSALM 42:1–2

Daily Prayer

Thank You, Father, for the armor You have provided. I will pray at all times—on every occasion, in every season—in the spirit, with all [manner of] prayer and entreaty. To that end I will keep alert and watch with strong purpose and perseverance, interceding on behalf of all the saints. My power, ability, and sufficiency are from You who qualified me as a minister and dispenser of a new covenant. Amen.

Day 3

The Climb for Perfectionism

Daily Scripture Verse

> I am the vine, you are the branches. He who abides in Me, and I in him, bears much fruit; for without Me you can do nothing.
>
> —JOHN 15:5

Striving for perfection has been a lifelong pursuit for me—an unsuccessful one at that! Growing up in a pastor's home, making good grades in school, studying classical piano, and being the church pianist didn't bring me satisfaction. Accomplishments didn't fill the hollow place in my soul. When I judged my spirituality by my church's standard of perfection, I was a colossal failure. With each infraction of their rules, I walked the aisle to get saved all over again or die and go to hell. Fear drove my quest for perfectionism, and I felt compelled to climb many treacherous mountains toward that impossible goal.

Life would be great when…but emptiness was always standing on the crest of each mountain forcing me to continue the laborious journey. Condemnation became my guide and depression my attendant. There was no one who could help me quiet the restlessness that dogged my every step. Religion failed me, and I was losing my fight to hold onto my faith—a faith that I didn't comprehend.

Marriage would surely be my great escape, but it merely reinforced my sense of failure—perfectionism was nowhere to be found. The futility of pretending that I had it all together became too grueling.

One day while I was sitting alone in my kitchen, I cried out to an invisible God for help. God answered, and I was wrapped in an unconditional love that compelled me to let down my walls and open the door of my heart.

Today, I have an intimate relationship with a loving heavenly Father. Jesus is my redeemer, my elder brother, and the Holy Spirit is my constant teacher and guide. I am accepted! There is no more condemnation. My life is the road that God walks.

Prayer is my safe place, my place of escape from the rigors of life. Prayer is my place of rest. Shut away with God in the secrecy of His pavilion I am free from the strife of tongues; I am healed; I am whole.

Talks with God may take many forms. We call it prayer. Prayer is not always talking; it also involves listening and journaling—writing is a wonderful method for recording your time with the One who knows you best, but loves you most. Private times alone with God are vital to your spiritual growth and emotional wholeness. When you pray, you experience the presence of God and fullness of joy, and you receive power to face the day. Jesus said, "Watch and pray that you enter not into temptation."

The LORD will perfect that which concerns me;
Your mercy, O LORD, endures forever;
Do not forsake the works of Your hands.
—PSALM 138:8

Daily Prayer

Father, in Jesus' name, I thank You for pouring forth Your love into my heart by the Holy Spirit whom You gave to me. This love of and for You is being perfected and completed in me, and perfect love casts out all fear.

Knowing that You are on my side, I decree that I am rooted deep in love and founded securely on love, and nothing is able to separate me from Your love, which is in Christ Jesus my Lord.

Day 4

Don't Focus on Your Weaknesses

Daily Scripture Verse

He said to me, "My grace is sufficient for you, for My strength is made perfect in weakness."

—2 CORINTHIANS 12:9

*I*n times of prayer, God will give revelation and bring about personal transformation. Your roles will take on vitality as your need for intimacy is fulfilled. Declare with boldness that the love of God is reigning supreme in your home, the peace of God rules your home, and the joy of the Lord is your strength. The light of God's Word dispels the darkness.

God isn't looking for perfectionism. He is looking for those who will walk after the Spirit, not after the flesh. You may never attain perfection, but you are God's woman or man, and He is not holding anything against you. When you do sin, you have an advocate with the Father. When you repent, He forgives you.

Have you been waiting a long time for your prayers to be answered? Have you grown weary, and are you tempted to give up? Prayer is essential to the life of the believer. Delight yourself in the Lord, and His desires will become yours. May His will be done on earth—in the life of your church, your family, and your

community, even as it is in heaven. Your time with God is never futile or wasted.

God will heal your emotional wounds, fulfill your unmet needs, and help you resolve your issues. You cannot attain perfectionism, a futile pursuit, but you can submit to a loving Father who cares for you and watches over you carefully. You can go back and face the disappointments and heartaches. When you face your fears, they fall helplessly behind you. You and God are a majority. You have the power and God-given ability to fulfill your destiny in spite of past mistakes. His Word will light your pathway! Our God is an awesome God!

> And we know that all things work together for good to those who love God, to those who are the called according to His purpose.
>
> —ROMANS 8:28

Daily Prayer

Father, I thank You for the Holy Spirit who brings all things to my remembrance. I will speak of excellent things, and the opening of my lips shall be for right things. My mouth shall speak truth; wickedness is an abomination to my lips. I keep my mouth that I might keep my life. May I always remember that he who has knowledge spares his words, and a man of understanding is of an excellent spirit. Death and life are in the power of the tongue. and they that love it shall eat the fruit thereof. I choose life that my generations might live unto righteousness. Amen.

Day 5

Don't Skip Your Quiet Times With God

Daily Scripture Verse

> Step out of the traffic! Take a long,
> loving look at me, your High God,
> above politics, above everything.
> —Psalm 46:10, The Message

*Q*uiet, contemplative prayer is a place of rest, an escape from the stress and weariness of everyday living. Here you are hidden away with God in the secrecy of His garden where you can shut out all your cares and concerns.

Talks with God may take many forms. Prayer is not always talking; it can be meditation, listening, and/or writing. Keep a prayer journal; record your precious moments with the One who knows you best, but loves you most.

Make up your mind to meet with the Father daily, praying and studying the Scriptures in sweet communion with the Holy Spirit. God yearns to reveal His heart to you. In these quiet moments with Him, your soul finds liberty—your heart vibrates with joy. Your soul will magnify the Lord, and your spirit will rejoice in God your Father throughout the day.

If you don't have a set time for fellowship with the Father, ask the Holy Spirit to give you His time for quiet meditations and prayer. The Father is calling His children to come away with Him.

> Truly my soul silently waits for God;
> From Him comes my salvation.
> He only is my rock and my salvation;

He is my defense;
I shall not be greatly moved.

—Psalm 62:1–2

Daily Prayer

*O God, You are my God, and I am fervently seeking You.
I thirst for You like a man lost in a desert where there is
no water. I have been in Your presence before and have
seen Your power and glory at work, but I cannot see You
now. But Your love is better to me than life, so I will continue to glorify You. I will praise You with my uplifted
hands for as long as I live. I will be satisfied only by You.
When I lie on my bed at night I remember Your goodness
to me. I think of You all night long. I cling to You, and
Your right hand holds me up. You have spread a banner
of love over my life.*

Day 1

United in Prayer for Our Nation

Daily Scripture Verse

> He who dwells in the secret place of the Most High
> Shall abide under the shadow of the Almighty....
> You shall not be afraid of the terror by night,
> Nor of the arrow that flies by day,
> Nor of the pestilence that walks in darkness,
> Nor of the destruction that lays waste at noonday.
> —PSALM 91:1, 5–6

It was a time of solitude when the heart was quiet and at peace. In the predawn, a full moon hung from a rose-tinted sky, and I stood mesmerized by God's music—unseen insects chirping, frogs croaking, birds singing, and geese squawking. A new day was dawning. Breathing deeply, I was filled with the presence of God. I had peace like a river. My heart was replete with thanksgiving as I drank in the beauty of God's creation.

Turning from the serenity of the calm waters of Lake Oconee, I remembered that tragic day, September 11, 2001, when our lives were changed forever. Terrifying events crashed into our normal daily routines, robbing us of our national security. Silently, with heavy hearts, we sat before our televisions viewing repeats of that terrible moment in history.

Terrorists who believed in a religion of hatred became our judge, jury, and executioner. Over the next few months we listened for the latest developments in our country, Afghanistan, and other nations. It was a dreadful day, but a day when our nation faced fear with faith, and the call to prayer was proclaimed and heard by fellow Americans. President Bush declared war against terrorism, and it is still a work in progress.

During a time of war everyone is needed; everyone can contribute. We who stay at home can pray, standing shoulder to shoulder in orderly array, clothed in God's armor, praying with all manner of prayer and entreaty. It is not the time to turn coward, give up, or lose heart; we are a people of prayer.

> Deliver me, O LORD, from evil men;
> Preserve me from violent men,
> Who plan evil things in their hearts;
> They continually gather together for war.
>
> —PSALM 140:1–2

Daily Prayer

Heavenly Father, thank You for our family and friends and Your bountiful supply. We are grateful for our country, the United States of America, the only country in the world founded upon religious freedom and Your Word. Thank You for our founding fathers, Lord, who looked to You for guidance to develop the kind of government that would be pleasing to You. May the light of Your Word run swiftly throughout our country, and may Your love burn brightly in our land. Give us a rebirth of freedom. We ask You to comfort those who mourn, and may there be peace on earth. Thank You for Your grace that is sufficient in every situation, in the name of Jesus. Amen.

Day 2

"God Will Bring Something Good Out of This Mess"

Daily Scripture Verse

> Hear my voice, O God, in my meditation;
> Preserve my life from fear of the enemy,

Hide me from the secret plots of the wicked,
From the rebellion of the workers of iniquity.
—Psalm 64:1–2

*I*n those first few weeks after the attack by terrorists on the United States, our churches were crowded and prayer groups flourished; we were a people united in prayer. Publicly we sang with one voice, "God bless America, land that I love. Stand beside her and guide her…"

The people of the world prayed for America. A pastor in Kenya called an all-night prayer meeting to pray for our president and our country. Another pastor from Kampala, Uganda, sent an e-mail to friends, revealing how God spoke to him from Psalm 64. "This battle will be won on our knees. I would encourage you to stay united in prayer for USA. God will bring something good out of this mess." From many lands they sent us assurance—they were praying for our president and his cabinet, asking God to help us in our time of need.

Christians from around the world continue to pray for America. Let us not forget! Let us not turn coward and lose heart! It is my prayer that the army of the Lord will remain in united prayer, a powerful weapon that has defeated and will defeat the plans of those opposed to freedom and righteousness. We who are called by the name of our God must respond as watchmen on the wall and remain alert, watching and praying. We were chosen for such a time as this.

United in prayer we stand declaring Jesus is Lord over the United States of America. We stand for freedom, goodness, mercy, and justice, and against the terrorist network—Satan's instruments of destruction. United in prayer we stand counting it all joy—the joy of the Lord is our strength, displacing fear and depression. United in prayer we stand, offering prayers with thanksgiving to the Father.[7]

The Lord brings the counsel of the nations [*terrorists*] to nought; He makes the thoughts and plans of the peoples of no effect. The counsel of the Lord stands forever, the thoughts of His heart through all generations.

—Psalm 33:10–11, amp

Daily Prayer

Father, in the name of Jesus, we praise You and offer up thanksgiving because the day of the Lord is near—Jesus is coming soon. Therefore, we will not fret or have any anxiety about the terrorism that is threatening the lives of those stationed on foreign soil and those of us who are at home. In this circumstance and in everything by prayer and petition [definite requests] with thanksgiving we continue to make our wants known to You. We ask that terrorism be stopped before it spreads to other cities around the world. We are established on righteousness in conformity with Your will and order. Amen.

Day 3

Humble Yourself—and Pray

Daily Scripture Verse

Great is our Lord, and mighty in power;
His understanding is infinite,
The Lord lifts up the humble;
He casts the wicked down to the ground.

—Psalm 147:5–6

*T*his morning we awoke to a winter wonderland—snow had blanketed our city. The snowfall was fluffy and

white, covering a multitude of imperfections. Everything looked beautiful, and as I was enjoying the view from my window the Holy Spirit began speaking to my heart.

The presidential election is over, and God's candidate has been positioned as He ordained. God heard the cries of His people. Everything looks beautiful, but when all the fluff has melted, we are still a divided nation, and the acrimony has not waned. This election exposed the extent of our national schism. Jesus said that a divided kingdom ends in ruin. A city or home divided against itself cannot stand (Matt. 12:25).

A mandate from the Holy Spirit is heard throughout our country. It is not abating but intensifying. Let us not relax and abort this prayer assignment.

> If My people who are called by My name will humble themselves, and pray and seek My face, and turn from their wicked ways, then I will hear from heaven, and will forgive their sin and heal their land.
> —2 Chronicles 7:14

Daily Prayer

> *Father, in Jesus' name, we thank You for the United States and its government. We pray for the men and women who are in positions of authority—the president, representatives, senators, judges, police personnel, as well as the governors and mayors and all others who are in authority over us in any way. We pray that the Spirit of God will rest upon them. Amen.*

Day 4

The Balm of Gilead

Daily Scripture Verse

> Therefore I exhort first of all that supplications,
> prayers, intercessions, and giving of thanks be made
> for all men, for kings and all who are in authority, that
> we may lead a quiet and peaceable life in all godliness
> and reverence.
>
> —1 Timothy 2:1–2

There is much work yet to be done in our nation. As intercessors, praying for the will of God to be done in our land, we must include all people, asking the Father for what they need and being thankful to Him. Let us lay aside our worldly ideologies and destroy every philosophy that exalts itself above the Word of God. God will do something awesome in our land if the church will persevere in prayer.

It takes someone to pray. God moves as we pray in faith…believing. Worship God, and let your words be few—talk the answers, not the problems. May God raise up intercessors who will surround our president with prayer.

Political parties do not impress God. He looks for particular men and women who will submit to His plans and purposes. He is looking for a particular group of people who will say, "Not my will, but Yours be done."

It is my prayer that the Balm of Gilead will blanket America and heal our land from sea to shining sea, just as the pure white snow blanketed our city and countryside.

Is there no balm in Gilead,
Is there no physician there?

Why then is there no recovery
For the health of the daughter of my people?

—JEREMIAH 8:22

Daily Prayer

*We ask that skillful and godly wisdom enter into the heart
of our president. We pray that discretion will watch over
him, that understanding will keep him and deliver him
from the way of evil and from evil men. Father, we ask
You to encompass the president with men and women
who make their hearts and ears attentive to godly counsel
and do that which is right in Your sight. In the name of
Jesus, amen.*[8]

Day 5

Prayer for Our World

Daily Scripture Verse

He who dwells in the secret place of the Most High
shall remain stable and fixed under the shadow of the
Almighty [Whose power no foe can withstand].

—PSALM 91:1, AMP

September 11, 2001, is a day that has changed our lives forever. Early that morning, while sitting at my desk preparing
for a week of writing and relaxation, I looked up, enjoying the
serene setting outside the French doors. The tranquil waters of
Lake Oconee looked soothing and refreshing. Unaware that our
country was under attack, I smiled as the white squirrel scampered along the ground underneath the hardwood trees.

Later that day I turned on the television and realized that
our sense of national security had been stripped from us. This

moment of time in our history made us aware of our vulnerability, and more people recognized their need for God and turned to prayer for strength and moral fortitude.

Several years ago, I had written a prayer to overcome fear of terrorism for those who traveled to other countries. Now I pray this prayer for the entire world, including the United States of America. As you and your family begin each day pray for one another, trusting God to hear and answer prayer.

> God reigns over the nations;
> God sits on His holy throne.

> —Psalm 47:8

Daily Prayer

Father God, we look to You, our refuge and our fortress, our God. On You we lean and rely, and in You we confidently trust. When we feel afraid, we will trust in You. Your truth and Your faithfulness are a shield and a buckler, and we will not fear the terror of the night or the arrow that flies by day. Thank You for giving Your angels charge over us to accompany and defend and preserve us in all our ways. Amen.

Day 1

Does God Call Us to Be Intercessors?

Daily Scripture Verse

Therefore we also pray always for you that our God would count you worthy of this calling, and fulfill all the good pleasure of His goodness and the work of faith with power, that the name of our Lord Jesus Christ may be glorified in you, and you in Him, according to the grace of our God and the Lord Jesus Christ.

—2 Thessalonians 1:11–12

Does God call certain individuals to be intercessors? The answer is both yes and no. Yes, you are called to "pray at all times (on every occasion, in every season) in the Spirit, with all [manner of] prayer and entreaty" (Eph. 6:18, AMP). No, the Bible does not list an office of "intercession."

Yet, God gives certain ones an extra measure of grace to pray, and often they become known as intercessors. I believe intercessors are in the ministry of helps, and of necessity we remain the hidden part of the body of Christ. Our assignment is to support those in public ministry.

The God-called intercessor captures the vision of the pastor and prayerfully enforces the triumphant victory of our Lord Jesus Christ. Unfortunately, when control issues are unsettled and misunderstandings arise, communication breaks down between the pastor and the intercessor. We are all human beings—people on the unending journey toward spiritual growth, and hopefully we are ever learning, growing, and achieving.

I do not pray for these alone, but also for those who will believe in Me through their word; that they all

may be one, as You, Father, are in Me, and I in You; that they also may be one in Us, that the world may believe that You sent me.

—JOHN 17:20–21

Daily Prayer

Father, in the name of Jesus, I pray for our families, declaring Your ways. You are faithful to answer. Teach us Your statutes, and make us understand Your precepts. We will meditate on Your wonderful works. Our souls melt with heaviness at times, so I ask You to strengthen us according to Your Word. Remove lying from us, and grant us Your law graciously. We have chosen the way of truth. Your judgments we lay before us; we cling to Your testimonies. O Lord, You will not put us to shame! We will run the course of Your commandments, for You are enlarging our hearts. Amen.

Day 2

Does God Give Intercessory Prayer Assignments?

Daily Scripture Verse

He [God] has delivered us from such a deadly peril, and he will deliver us. On him we have set our hope that he will continue to deliver us, as you help us by your prayers.

—2 CORINTHIANS 1:10–11, NIV

God has not given us intercessory prayer assignments because we are spiritual giants who have attained spiritual maturity in one swift moment of time. He called us by His grace and according to His purpose to be His agents of prayer.

Prayer is a lifestyle that has to be learned and practiced in the school of the spirit. God placed apostles, prophets, evangelists, pastors, and teachers in the church for the equipping of the saints for the work of ministry, for the edifying of the body of Christ.

God brings us into completeness of personality, and our prayer life becomes more effectual when we are no longer subject to every wind of doctrine. As useful members of the body of Christ, we learn to submit to one another, to speak the truth in love, and to grow up in all things into Him who is the head.

> He Himself gave…that we should no longer be children, tossed to and fro and carried about with every wind of doctrine…but, speaking the truth in love, may grow up in all things into Him who is the head.
>
> —EPHESIANS 4:11, 14–15

Daily Prayer

Father, thank You for comforting us and assuring us of Your divine intervention as we walk this journey here on earth. We dwell, remain, and settle down under the shadow (defense, protection) of the Almighty. We will say of the Lord that You are our refuge, our place of protection. You are our God, true and faithful. You are our place of security. You did not give us a spirit of fear—but a spirit of power, of love, of calm and well-balanced mind, of discipline, and of self-control. In Your name we bind our emotions to the control of the Holy Spirit and go forth with confidence. Amen.

Day 3

Transformation of the Soul Required

Daily Scripture Verse

> We also eagerly wait for the Savior, the Lord Jesus Christ, who will transform our lowly body that it may be conformed to His glorious body.
>
> —PHILIPPIANS 3:20–21

Growing up is an ongoing process. The Word of God divides soul and spirit, exposing the excess baggage that gets in the way of learning to pray effectively. It is painful to let go of a compulsive need to rescue and control others, a need to feel significant or be accepted, and other unresolved issues. When we yield to the ministry of transformation by the Holy Spirit, soulish prayers of manipulation are replaced with "not my will, but Yours be done."

One of the benefits of praying for others is that we are in a position to receive emotional healing and experience spiritual maturation. Even though God helps us work out our own salvation with fear and trembling, we make mistakes along the way. My prayer is always that my mistakes will not impede the progress of others.

In the school of prayer we encounter tests—wonderful opportunities for growth. In the early stages of hearing God's voice, we are tempted to run ahead of Him and even abort our prayer assignments. As our prayer life develops, another stumbling block to be avoided is pride. We overestimate ourselves and underestimate others. If you fall into this trap, repent, strengthen your trembling knees, and learn from your mistakes.

A great hindrance to successful prayer is focusing on changing or fixing those for whom we pray. I know wonderful people who have fallen prey to this need to fix others, even their pastors! When they can't make their prayers happen, they depart, blaming others for their "prayer failure," and souls remain in disrepair. God wants to develop character in His children, not extend deficits.

> Not that I have already attained, or am already perfected;
> but I press on, that I may lay hold of that for which Christ
> Jesus has also laid hold of me....I press toward the goal for
> the prize of the upward call of God in Christ Jesus.
> —Philippians 3:12, 14

Daily Prayer

> Holy Spirit, You are our liberator! Now the Lord is the
> Spirit, and where the Spirit of the Lord is, there is liberty.
> But we all, with unveiled face, beholding as in a mirror
> the glory of the Lord, are being transformed into the same
> image from glory to glory, just as by the Spirit of the Lord.
> The grace of the Lord Jesus Christ, the love of God, and
> the communion of the Holy Spirit are with me! Amen.

Day 4

From the Intercessor's Corner

Daily Scripture Verse

> Then those who gladly received his word were bap-
> tized; and that day about three thousand souls were
> added to them. And they continued steadfastly in the
> apostles' doctrine and fellowship, in the breaking of
> bread, and in prayers.
> —Acts 2:41–42

*I*n his book *Prayer: Key to Revival*, Pastor David Yonggi Cho of Seoul, South Korea, asks the question, "Are you ready for your church to enter into a powerful ministry in prayer so that your neighborhood, city or state knows the power that resides in your church? If this is your desire and you will do anything and pay any price, then get ready for God to dramatically change your life and ministry, bringing you into a new dimension of power."[9]

We can apply this principle to our God-given prayer assignments. Are we willing to pay the price to see a demonstration of the power of God in our lives and in the lives of those for whom we are praying? There are nuggets of truth throughout the Bible that reveal the price we have to pay. Acts 2:42 is one of those nuggets. The new believers *accepted* and *welcomed* the message preached, and they were baptized. They did not say, "Oh, well, now that we are born again we can run on our way." They *steadfastly persevered*, *devoting* themselves *constantly* to the instruction and fellowship of the apostles, to the breaking of bread (including the Lord's Supper), and prayers.

To pray effectively we must balance our prayer with the study of the Word. Rather than praying for God to answer your bidding, His will is revealed to you.

> For you have need of endurance, so that after you have done the will of God, you may receive the promise.
> —HEBREWS 10:36

Daily Prayer

> *Father, we rejoice because we have been justified by faith and have peace with You through our Lord Jesus Christ. By whom also we have access by faith into this grace wherein we stand and rejoice in hope of the glory of God. We shout glory to God in the heavenly heights, peace to*

*all men and women on earth who please You. This is the
day that You have made, and we rejoice in You, God our
Savior, in the name of Jesus. Amen.*

Day 5

Intercessory Visits With God

Daily Scripture Verse

You will show me the path of life;
In Your presence is fullness of joy;
At Your right hand are pleasures forevermore.

—PSALM 16:11

A visit with God, enjoying His presence, gives us opportunity for fruitful growth in the faith. E. W. Kenyon wrote, "The call to prayer is the Father's invitation to visit with Him. This is more than the consciousness of a great need that often drives us to intercession."[10]

When we neglect our visits with our Father, the needs of people become so overwhelming, and we are pushed beyond our limits. Respond to the Master's call, "Come to Me, all you who labor and are heavy laden, and I will give you rest."

You have a divine destiny. God chose you before the foundation of the world to be His very own, and He set boundaries round about you to keep you on target. It is my belief that this destiny is connected to the destiny of others. We are a household of prayer with individual and collective prayer assignments.

Come to Me, all you who labor and are heavy laden,
and I will give you rest. Take My yoke upon you and
learn from Me, for I am gentle and lowly in heart, and

you will find rest for your souls. For My yoke is easy
and My burden is light.

—MATTHEW 11:28–30

Daily Prayer

Glorious Father, I ask You, the God of our Lord Jesus
Christ, to give us the Spirit of wisdom and revelation. I
pray that whatever we do or say will be as a true represen-
tative of the Lord Jesus, and together we will give thanks
through Him to You, Most High God. Father, I thank
You for calling us to be Your ambassadors of good will here
on this earth. Amen.

Day 1

A Mother of Faith

Daily Scripture Verse

Therefore my heart is glad, and my glory rejoices;
My flesh also will rest in hope.

—PSALM 16:9

My mother, Donnis Brock Griffin, prayed daily for her family, and it was her delight to share about meeting the Lord and how God directed her life. Dressed in her Christmas skirt and sweater with the glow of the lights reflected on her joy-filled face, surrounded by her children and grandchildren, she once again told us the story that never grows old. We listened with rapt attention to the words of this mother of faith.

One day a young minister came to preach in our village, and my pastor insisted that I meet him. We began seeing each other. When this itinerate preacher moved on, I never expected to hear from him again. But before long, I was receiving romantic letters, declaring his love for me. Yes, your grandfather is a romantic!

Well, one day he came back to preach a revival where I was the church pianist, and we saw each other every night. One moonlit night we sat gently swinging on the porch swing back and forth. Of course, you know what happened; he asked me to marry him. Shortly, we said goodnight. Preparing for bed, I began praying, "O God, tell me what to do. I've only known Buck a few months. He doesn't even own a car. Show me what to do."

The next morning just before waking, I had a dream. I heard my mother's voice saying, "Buck has

called you. Now you call him." Startled, I awoke and ran to the kitchen. "Mama, why did you say that? What did you mean?" Low and behold, she hadn't even called me to get up. Then I heard that still small voice that is so precious to me, "Donnis, remember, you prayed."

Then I knew—God was directing my steps. Your grandfather and I went through valleys and walked on mountain peaks, we've experienced heartaches and joys, but I've never doubted, never questioned God. I've lived all these years knowing that I am in the will of God for my life. The heavenly Father knew Buck and me before the foundation of the world, and He brought us together as husband and wife for His purpose. Wait on God to reveal your life partner, and fulfill your destiny.

Donnis Brock Griffin went to be with the Lord at the age of eighty-one. She and her husband, Rev. A. H. "Buck" Griffin, were married almost sixty-four years at the time of her death. They served as pastors for more than forty years and continued in ministry the remainder of her life.

I wait for the LORD, my soul waits,
And in His word I do hope.

—Psalm 130:5

Daily Prayer

Father, I thank You for sending Jesus. In Him all the fullness of the Deity lives in bodily form, and I have been given fullness in Christ, who is the head over every power and authority. My completeness or fulfillment is not in a mate, but in Christ Jesus, my Lord. I am complete in Him. I desire a Christian mate, and pray for Your will to be done in my life.

Day 2

A Son Redeemed

Daily Scripture Verse

> And it shall come to pass in the last days, saith God,
> I will pour out of my Spirit upon all flesh: and your
> sons and your daughters shall prophesy, and your
> young men shall see visions, and your old men shall
> dream dreams.
>
> —ACTS 2:17, KJV

The young man stood before the congregation—his face beaming—the light in his eyes rejoicing the heart of the people. He began to speak, and a silence fell over those who had come to hear the guest speaker.

He began: "It took a trip to prison for me to get right with God. My grandmother and mother prayed for me all my life. My dad bailed me out of many situations from the time I was a teenager. But the day came when I had to suffer the consequences of the wrong choices I had made over a period of twenty-eight years. There was no one I could blame except myself.

"At first I was belligerent…doing what I had to do, but no more. They told me when to go to bed, when to get up, and when I could eat. They controlled my every waking moment. But in prison, one of two things happens—either you become a more skillful criminal, or you get close to God. I got close to my God."

He continued by saying, "When you pray, God works. Parents, I admonish you, never quit praying and believing God for the salvation of your children. Never give up. Replace your

fears and worries with the Scripture, those promises God has given concerning your children. One day when my mother was reading the Book of Acts, she began to pray that her children would walk in truth. She prayed prophetically: 'It is written that if I believe on the Lord Jesus Christ, I and my entire household shall be saved (Acts 16:31). I thank You, Father, for the salvation of my children and grandchildren. In the name of Jesus, I bind my children's feet to paths of righteousness. I demolish the power of false pride and loose ungodly reasoning that would exalt itself above the knowledge of God. The promise [of the gift of the Holy Spirit] is unto me, and to my children, and to all that are afar off, even as many as the Lord our God shall call (Acts 2:39).'

"Nothing is impossible to him who believes. Now I am praying this same prayer for my children. They suffered through my years of addiction, and I am praying that every decision they make will draw them nearer to receiving Jesus. He has given unto me the ministry of reconciliation, and while I am waiting upon Him, I shout, 'Hallelujah! My God reigns.' God will restore what the enemy has stolen for His glory. He never fails one word of His promise. Never turn coward or give up. Your children belong to God."

> But thus saith the LORD, Even the captives of the mighty shall be taken away, and the prey of the terrible shall be delivered: for I will contend with him that contendeth with thee, and I will save thy children.
>
> —ISAIAH 49:25, KJV

Daily Prayer

> *Father, in the name of Jesus, I pray for my family's salvation. Teach us Your statutes, and make us understand Your precepts, and we will meditate on Your wonderful*

works. Our souls melt with heaviness at times, so I ask You to strengthen us according to Your Word. Remove lying from us, and grant us Your law graciously. We have chosen the way of truth. We cling to Your testimonies. O Lord, You will not put us to shame! We will run the course of Your commandments, for You are enlarging our hearts. Amen.

Day 3

Determine Your Identity

Daily Scripture Verse

For we are His workmanship, created in Christ Jesus for good works, which God prepared beforehand that we should walk in them.

—EPHESIANS 2:10

Our true identity comes into focus when we become acquainted with and understand God. Knowing God enables you to unite with the intercession of Jesus and yield to the leadership of the Holy Spirit. Your spirit, soul, and body unite to love the Lord your God with all your being, and your neighbor as yourself.

Do you identify yourself as "intercessor"? Identity must go much deeper than a title. Intercession is not to be taken lightly, and knowing who you are in Christ is crucial to praying effectively. When one becomes a Christian he remains emotionally tied to unhealed hurts, unmet needs, disappointments, broken promises, regrets, and unfulfilled dreams. An identity rooted in the past can be striped away, and a new identity emerges.

In Christ a great exchange is possible. Jesus identified with

you in your helpless state of transgression, and now you can identify with Him in His resurrection power and the fellowship of His sufferings.

You are God's workmanship re-created in Christ Jesus. You were chosen by God, chosen for the high calling of priestly work, chosen to be a holy people, God's instruments to do His work and speak out for Him, to tell others of the night-and-day difference He made for you (See 1 Peter 2:9.)

When the eyes of your understanding are opened and you put on the new man, the new identity is established and you see others through the eyes of love. Effective intercessory prayer is born out of a heart of compassion. One night I was awakened by a sneering voice, "Who do you think you are to teach others to pray?" Without hesitation I answered, "I am a daughter of the Most High God." Knowing your true identity gives you assurance and boldness to stand against the accusations of the enemy.

> But whoever did want him,
>> who believed he was who he claimed
>> and would do what he said,
> He made to be their true selves,
>> their child-of-God selves.
> —JOHN 1:12, THE MESSAGE

Daily Prayer

Father, we have received Christ Jesus the Lord, so we will walk in Him, rooted and built up in Him, established in the faith and joyfully abounding in it. Love is our foundation, and we pray that Christ will be at home in us. May we be rooted and grounded in love, able to comprehend with all the saints what is the width and length and depth and height—to know the love of Christ which passes

knowledge, that we may be filled with all the fullness of God, and walk as Jesus walked in love, in harmony and unity with one another. Amen.

Day 4

Determine Your Integrity

Daily Scripture Verse

The integrity of the upright will guide them,
But the perversity of the unfaithful will destroy them.
—Proverbs 11:3

Determine in your heart to live a life of integrity shaped by righteousness—God's ways of doing and being right. Rigidity gives way to flexibility, and your desires will be congruent with God's desires. Your prayer life takes on consistency as you cast down wrong thought patterns, religious dogmas, and wrong concepts that are protected by strongholds. Integrity, rather than your feelings, will govern your prayer life. You are complete in Christ. To experience the completeness found only in Christ Jesus we must walk in integrity.

Intercessors can be the catalyst of salvation for a troubled church. I have lived long enough to experience times of refreshing and times of unrest in the churches where we have attended. I watched and learned from my mentors who were strong intercessors of firm integrity. They remained faithful and loyal to the vision even when pastors fell. The prayers of the righteous supported those who had to make unpopular decisions and paved the pathway for many to return to the fold. New members were added to the church, and the churches are stronger than ever.

Many of us pride ourselves on our honesty, but the need to control our environment drives us to extreme, rigid tactics that force separation. Dishonesty seems to be inherent in people who grew up in dysfunctional family systems. They were taught to keep family secrets that required them to tell glib lies to extended family members, bosses, teachers, and neighbors. We are to put away falsity and speak the truth in love.

Sometimes a need for acceptance gives place to pretense and compromise, and Satan gains access. We may hedge and skirt the truth to avoid hurting others and try to shield them from truth that would set them free. The truth can be painful, and our prayers according to the will of God are capable of sustaining an individual until they come to terms and resolve their issues.

A godly level of integrity will drive out contrariness and function as a compass in your prayer life.

Let integrity and uprightness preserve me,
For I wait for You.

—PSALM 25:21

Daily Prayer

Father, thank You for the Holy Spirit who helps me love without hypocrisy. I abhor what is evil and cling to what is good. I will be kindly affectionate to others with brotherly love, in honor giving preference to others, not lagging in diligence, fervent in spirit, serving the Lord. I rejoice in hope, I am patient in tribulation, and I will continue steadfast in prayer—distributing to the needs of the saints, given to hospitality. I am an imitator of my heavenly Father in the name of Jesus. Amen.

Day 5

Determine Your Influence

Daily Scripture Verse

So I sought for a man among them who would make a wall, and stand in the gap before Me on behalf of the land, that I should not destroy it; but I found no one.

—Ezekiel 22:30

W hen you begin praying for others, your influence expands and people are drawn to you. Keep your perspective and lift up the name of Jesus, not the effectiveness of your prayers. You won't have to broadcast your commitment to pray. You are a living epistle read of all men.

Each intercessor determines his or her influence. Determining your influence will enable you to assume responsibility for personal decisions and your behavior. It has been said that you and God are a majority, but you are not an island unto yourself. You are the link between past and future generations. Take your place, build up the wall, and stand in the gap before God for your posterity. Break the power of iniquity that was passed down from your forefathers, and withstand the judgment of God (Ezek. 22:30–31). Put on behavior that is becoming to the Lord Jesus Christ.

Spreading love, showing respect, giving a sincere smile, offering a hand, or simply being available to listen leaves a lasting impression. Our presence has an affect on children, grandchildren, spouses, neighbors, and friends. "You are the only Jesus some people will ever see."

We are all interconnected. The girl at the checkout counter, the man at the dry cleaners, the carpet cleaner, hairstylist, park-

ing lot attendant...brief encounters where your influence is felt. Are you living a lifestyle of prayer? A transformed life gives hope to others who have believed that they could never change.

The prophet Daniel was an intercessor who maintained his identity. He was given another name and held a prominent position in the king's court, but he always referred to himself by his true name, Daniel. He approached his superiors and maintained his integrity, and God gave him favor and compassion in the sight of the officials. Your identification is in Christ Jesus. You are an overcomer, an ambassador, holding out to others the Word of life. Daniel's lifestyle influenced others to believe in the one true God. Your lifestyle of prayer will turn many from darkness to light, from Satan to God.

> Now therefore, our God, hear the prayer of Your servant, and his supplications, and for the Lord's sake cause Your face to shine on Your sanctuary, which is desolate....O Lord, hear! O Lord, forgive! O Lord, listen and act! Do not delay for Your own sake, my God, for Your city and Your people are called by Your name.
>
> —Daniel 9:17, 19

Daily Prayer

> *Father, in the name of Jesus, I shall go to all to whom You send me, and whatever You command me, I shall speak. I will not be afraid of their faces, for You are with me to deliver me. Whenever I feel afraid, I will trust in You. I will praise Your Word, in You I have put my trust; I will not fear; what can man do to me? You have spoken, and my faith is in You. I can do all things through Christ who strengthens me. Amen.*

Day 1

The Intercessor

Daily Scripture Verse

> Son of man, I have made you a watchman for the house of Israel; therefore hear a word from My mouth, and give them warning from Me.
>
> —EZEKIEL 3:17

What is an intercessor? An intercessor is one who intervenes between parties with a view to reconciling differences. He could be called a mediator. My friend Minister Belinda Campbell describes an intercessor as one called to link God's mercy to human needs.

God looks in each generation for one person who will pray for the deliverance and salvation of his family members. My mother, Donnis Brock Griffin, carried the mantle of intercession for her family. Her parents, brothers, and sisters were born again. God intervened, and the ministry begun in her generation continues today in the lives of her children, grandchildren, nephews, nieces, and their children. This mantle of intercession was passed to my sister and me, and now our children are receiving the mantle to pray for others.

Order your steps in God's Word by applying His principles, and join with other believers to stand "in the gap" and make a difference for God in the world. God, who reconciled us to Himself through Christ, gave us the ministry of reconciliation. Prayer prepares the road to reconciliation. The intercessor stands before God asking for His mercy, which will triumph over judgment. Sin has already been judged, and when a person sins, judgment comes with it. But your prayers will bring

divine intervention in situations in the lives of those for whom you are praying.

Intercession requires patience, a mighty weapon in prayer. We pray, then wait on the Lord, praising Him and giving Him the glory, knowing that we are praying according to His will, purpose, and plan on behalf of a loved one, friend, or foe. Only God knows how and when to intervene; we know it is His will that all men be saved and come to the knowledge of the truth. He alone knows how to penetrate mind-sets and draw individuals to Himself.

Submit to the leadership of the Holy Spirit and the Word of God when you pray. Separate soulish emotions from spiritual prompting, and pray. Your prayers will make a difference!

> Let not mercy and truth forsake you;
> Bind them around your neck,
> Write them on the tablet of your heart,
> And so find favor and high esteem
> In the sight of God and man.
>
> —PROVERBS 3:3–4

Daily Prayer

> *I thank my God always concerning you for the grace of God that was given to you by Christ Jesus, that you were enriched in everything by Him in all utterance and all knowledge, even as the testimony of Christ was confirmed in you, so that you come short in no gift, eagerly waiting for the revelation of our Lord Jesus Christ, who will confirm you to the end that you may be blameless in the day of our Lord Jesus Christ. God is faithful, by whom you were called into the fellowship of His Son, Jesus Christ our Lord. Amen.*

Day 2

The Team Needs a Leader

Daily Scripture Verse

Those who are wise shall shine
Like the brightness of the firmament,
And those who turn many to righteousness
Like the star forever and ever.

—DANIEL 12:3

It is almost self-evident—any team needs a leader! God spoke to me in an unspiritual setting. My husband and I sat in the living room watching a sports show. Needing to feel connected, I asked questions that were answered with measured patience.

Silently, I wondered why intelligent beings wanted to play this hazardous game of football. They deliberately slammed into each other, knocked each other down, and fell in massive tangled piles. With my husband's help, I began to have a little understanding about the offensive and defensive strategy as it unfolded.

To my amazement, the linemen suddenly became intercessors and those in the ministry of helps. They were in position, ready to charge the opposing line and open a path for their backfield to break through. Behind them stood the quarterback (the apostle, prophet, evangelist, pastor, and teacher), who was responsible for properly reading the defense and calling the correct offensive plays.

Regardless of how well the linemen played, since they neither called the plays nor carried the ball, they were limited in their capacity to win. Without the well-prepared, mentally alert, able-bodied quarterback, theirs was virtually an impossible task.

The quarterback could not lead his team to victory without the proper preparation and willingness to accept and follow the instructions of his coach.

The light dawned! As the president of Word Ministries, I acknowledged my prayer slump and repented for transferring personal blame and condemnation to my teammates. The real fault was mine for having neglected my privilege to spend time conferring directly with my "Divine Coach" and to carefully follow His game plan.

In the body of Christ we are team members, working together in harmony with the Holy Spirit and one another. Without prayer there is no spiritual success, and we need every member, including intercessors, working together for harmony in the church.

Our foundation is the Word; our standard, the banner of love; our clothing, humility. Through the power of prayer we make it possible for the church to be closely joined and firmly knit together by the joints and ligaments with which it is supplied. The quarterback cannot win the game by himself—he needs the team working together shoulder to shoulder in orderly array.

> But, speaking the truth in love, may grow up in all things into Him who is the head—Christ—from whom the whole body, joined and knit together by what every joint supplies, according to the effective working by which every part does its share, causes growth of the body for the edifying of itself in love.
> —Ephesians 4:15–16

Daily Prayer

> *Teach us, O Lord, the way of Your statutes, and we will keep it to the end. Give us understanding, and we will*

keep Your laws. We will observe it with our whole heart. In the name of Jesus I bind our feet to the path of Your commandments, and we delight in it. Incline our hearts to Your testimonies and not to covetousness. Turn away our eyes from looking at worthless things, and revive us in Your way. Establish Your Word to Your children who are devoted to You. Turn away our reproach, which we dread for Your judgments are good. Behold, we long for Your precepts; revive us in Your righteousness. Father, I thank You for new ideas and new revelation. Amen.

Day 3

Prayer Support

Daily Scripture Verse

> Could you not watch with Me one hour? Watch and pray, lest you enter into temptation. The spirit indeed is willing, but the flesh is weak.
>
> —Matthew 26:40–41

Jesus is our example, and there was a time when He asked for prayer support. Most often He prayed alone, and the supernatural pervaded the natural, the heavens opened, and the will of God was revealed as the natural was changed into the supernatural and the Father was glorified. In His hour of greatest need, however, Jesus called three of His closest disciples to accompany Him, requesting that they stay awake and pray.

They failed Him—just as we often do. How sad that the Holy Spirit has to pass us by and look for others who will submit to His gentle nudging to pray. Intercessory prayer groups can be a great asset and pillar of the church. If prayer groups

are to be effective, it is necessary that a minister maintain close contact with the prayer group leader by giving (and receiving) wise counsel. A group that is led by the pastor himself has direct counsel and knowledge of the specific areas of concern in the church. Other churches have appointed prayer group leaders. The Elder of Prayer in one church where I have ministered provides a written report for her pastors each week.

The pastor is aware of details that the intercessors may or may not need to know, and a prayer report may confirm or clear the way for another level of church growth. The mistake made by some ministers is that of depending solely on one or two persons to pray and hear from God for the direction of the ministry.

When this happens, the responsibility for the church guidance has been shifted from the God-appointed leader to a member of the flock. In this circumstance, the other person is placed in a position to dominate and usurp authority—falling into the error of dictating another's pathway of ministry.

So often we fail because we do not wait on the plan of God, or fail to follow divine lines of authority. Inadvertently, we give others the power to oversee the vision of a congregation, and as a result, both pastors and laymen are often wounded. A pastor is responsible to keep himself spiritually built up, and the intercessors are those who hold up his arms, support him, and reinforce his prayers.

> Continue earnestly in prayer, being vigilant in it with thanksgiving; meanwhile praying also for us, that God would open to us a door for the word, to speak the mystery of Christ…as I ought to speak.
> —COLOSSIANS 4:2–4

Father, we believe in our hearts that You raised Jesus from the dead, and we affirm that Jesus is Lord over our spirits, souls, and bodies. As His representatives, we are anointed to bring good news to the suffering and afflicted. His anointing comforts the broken-hearted, and we announce liberty to the captives. The time of God's favor has come to all those who mourn. Father God, You planted us like strong and graceful oaks for Your own glory and anointed us to rebuild the ancient ruins, reviving them though they have lain there many generations. We thank You for forgiving all our iniquities and healing all our diseases. We decree that our families and future generations shall come to the knowledge of the truth and be saved. We offer this prayer in the name of Jesus. Amen.

Day 4

Direction Is Important

Daily Scripture Verse

Therefore if there is any consolation in Christ, if any comfort of love, if any fellowship of the Spirit, if any affection and mercy, fulfill my joy by being like-minded, having the same love, being of one accord, of one mind.

—Philippians 2:1–2

The intercessory prayer group is often an open door for the youngest of Christians. It is wise to require preparation classes before anyone is included in an intercessory prayer group. This can be a safe place, especially in a large congregation, for a

young Christian to be trained in the ways of God if that person is willing to follow the guidelines of the group.

Where there is direction and harmony, unity prevails. Understanding the vision, and submission to one another, insures answered prayer. Prayer will bring spiritual growth and emotional healing to a congregation. Individual and corporate prayer will bring us into a more intimate relationship with God, the Father, who lives in us all. The prayer of binding and loosing can usher in the anointing to crush, smash, and annihilate the strategies of the enemy.

In our prayer groups we learn to cooperate with one another, and we have opportunities for growth. Honesty in prayer groups requires us to confess our shortcomings and sins to God and to one another. Then, we pray for one another that we all may be healed and restored to a spiritual tone of mind and heart.

> And I will give you the keys of the kingdom of heaven, and whatever you bind on earth will be bound in heaven, and whatever you loose on earth will be loosed in heaven.
>
> —MATTHEW 16:19

Daily Prayer

Father, I will not perish because of a lack of knowledge. My delight is in the law of the Lord, and on Your law I meditate day and night. I accept Your words, turn my ear to wisdom, apply my heart to understand, and call out for insight and understanding. I look for it as for silver and search for it as for hidden treasure. Then I will understand the fear of the Lord and find knowledge of God. In the name of Jesus, I choose Your instruction instead of silver, and knowledge rather than choice gold. Amen.

Day 5

The Heart of God

Daily Scripture Verse

> I will dwell in them and walk among them. I will be
> their God, and they shall be My people.
> —2 CORINTHIANS 6:16

The world around me is still asleep; I haven't even heard a car go by. I embrace the quietness of this moment and know that God is here. He is the One who never leaves or forsakes us. All day, every day, our God dwells in us and walks among us. He has promised that He will be our God, and we will be His people. Waiting on the Lord, I sense that He is imparting His desire for all people everywhere. It is His desire that all men be saved and come to the knowledge of the truth.

Intercessors from many countries are praying for every tribe and language and people and nation because with His blood, Jesus purchased men for God (Rev. 5:9). There is power in the prayer of agreement, whether we are gathered in the same room or praying from around the world.

God redeemed us, brought us back to Himself through the sacrifice of His Son. And God has given us the task of reconciling people to Him. For God was in Christ, reconciling the world to Himself, no longer counting people's sins against them.

We may not all agree on doctrine, but we can agree with God's Word that declares His desire for all men to be saved. Let us unite! Jesus prayed that we would be one even as He and the Father are one. Praise God, strongholds that have separated us are coming down and labels are becoming less important as we focus on the kingdom of God and His righteousness. We are

brothers and sisters, comrades in the army of the Lord. Let's pray for the healing of the nations at every level, lasting peace, and righteous governments. Clothed in the armor of God, we are enforcing the triumphant victory Jesus won at Calvary.

God, my Father, has captured my heart. The prayer assignment is monumental, but Jesus works with us. We have two divine intercessors who cannot fail. The Holy Spirit helps us pray, and Jesus always lives to make intercession for us.

> Therefore He is also able to save to the uttermost those who come to God through Him, since He always lives to make intercession for them.
>
> —HEBREWS 7:25

Daily Prayer

Father, the love You define in 1 Corinthians 13 is my greatest aim, and I ask also for the special abilities the Holy Spirit gives. I believe on the name of Your Son, Jesus Christ, and I commit to love others just as I love myself, because You first loved me. God, You are love, and when I live in love, I am living with You and You live in me. As I live with Christ, my love grows more perfect and complete. Thank You for loving me. In the name of Jesus, amen.

Day 1

How Do You Identify Yourself?

Daily Scripture Verse

> You are a chosen generation, a royal priesthood, a holy
> nation, His own special people, that you may proclaim
> the praises of Him who called you out of darkness into
> His marvelous light.
>
> —1 Peter 2:9

*P*reparing for a seminar where I was to speak, I began to
pray starting at the second verse of Ephesians chapter one.
Sitting in my usual spot with my beloved Bible, the first verse
leaped off the page, calling me to attention. Paul's name faded,
and I saw "Germaine, an apostle…" Before you decide that I
am a self-appointed apostle, please read on. Protesting, I asked,
"Whatever does this mean?"

Out of nowhere a question was hurled at me. Do you know
who you are? Well, of course I do. No, you don't understand;
who do you think you are? This seemed like a voice from my
childhood, often asked when I had displeased one of my parents. Then, I answered, "I'm a daughter of the Most High God."
Good answer, good beginning! The accusing voice stopped.

Paul's letter addresses the church of Jesus Christ. In this
first verse Paul gives us a bold statement that carries with it a
tone of authority. Ephesians could be called a book of wisdom
for everyday living and what Paul is about to write is important
to the lifestyle of the believer. He prepares us to recognize our
role as a believer in the Lord Jesus Christ. He understands from
experience the daily struggles against an enemy who schemes to
steal our confidence and defeat our faith.

Without apology, Paul designates himself as an apostle

of the Lord Jesus Christ. He knew who he was in Christ and understood his divine appointment and destiny. His declaration established this letter as official, sealed with God's approval. Do you know your position in Christ—do you relate to Paul's position in ministry? How do you identify yourself?

> Am I not an apostle? Am I not free? Have I not seen Jesus Christ our Lord? Are you not my work in the Lord? If I am not an apostle to others, yet doubtless I am to you. For you are the seal of my apostleship in the Lord.
>
> —1 CORINTHIANS 9:1–2

Daily Prayer

> Father, when I open my eyes each morning I shall declare that this is the day You have made. You knew me before I was formed within my mother's womb; before I was born You sanctified me and appointed me as Your witness to the world. I was created for a specific and very special purpose. In the name of Jesus and with the help of the Holy Spirit, I shall fulfill my destiny. Amen.

Day 2

Special Messengers

Daily Scripture Verse

> Through Him we have received grace and apostleship for obedience to the faith among all nations for His name, among whom you also are the called of Jesus Christ.
>
> —ROMANS 1:5–6

You are beloved of God, called to be saints!

Paul's family background, education, and natural abilities did not qualify him to be an ambassador of Jesus Christ. God called him in compliance with the counsel of His will. If you are in Christ, you are a new creation, a minister of reconciliation, an ambassador of Christ, God making His appeal as it were through you. You are Christ's personal representative—His special messenger by the will of God!

God did not call Paul because of his exemplary lifestyle. Before his conversion he was a religious zealot who was rigid in his beliefs. He lived by the letter of the law, and punished anyone when it was in his power to do so. Saul had an encounter with Jesus Christ. He was on his way to Damascus to find more followers of the Way for the purpose of arresting them. At the outskirts of Damascus, he was blinded by a flash of light, and he heard a voice, saying, "Saul, Saul, why are you out to get Me?" It was Jesus! He told him to go into the city, and someone would come and tell him what to do next.

Saul was blind for three whole days. He refused to eat or drink anything. A believer by the name of Ananias was told in a vision where he was to go and that he would find Saul praying. Ananias couldn't believe what the Lord was saying—this had to be a bad dream. When he protested, the Lord said, "Don't argue. Go! I have picked him as my personal representative to Gentiles, kings, and Jews. I am about to show him what he's in for—the hard suffering that goes with this job."

Ananias obeyed the Lord, found the house where Saul was staying, and laid hands on him. Instantly, Saul could see again! From that day until the end of his life, he followed the plan of God and was used as a very special messenger to take the gospel of Christ around the world. And so are you, a very special messenger, an ambassador of Jesus Christ!

Now then, we are ambassadors for Christ, as though God were pleading through us.

—2 Corinthians 5:20

Daily Prayer

God, You called us into fellowship with Your Son, Jesus Christ our Lord, and You are faithful. You called us to this through the gospel that we might share in the glory of our Lord Jesus Christ. You saved us and chose us for this holy work, not because we deserved it, but because that was Your plan long before the world began—to show Your love and kindness to us through Christ. The One who calls us is faithful, and He will do it.

Day 3

The Answer to Someone's Need

Daily Scripture Verse

Yet who knows whether you have come to the kingdom for such a time as this?

—Esther 4:14

Your conversion was unique and special; you have a divine destiny. When Satan reminds you of bad things you have done and tries to convince you that God could never use you, remember Paul, who persecuted the church of God beyond measure and wasted it. (See Galatians 1:13.) He was God's answer to the Gentiles, and through his ministry a great mystery has been revealed. Gentiles are included in the plan of God. God created you for such a time as this, for this hour. You are the answer to someone's need. Out of your inmost being flows healing rivers, and others will know that there is hope.

Because you live, lives are different. Your influence is essential. While Jesus was on the earth, He was the light of the world. He has returned to the Father, and now you are the light drawing others to a place of hope and salvation.

> Do all things without complaining and disputing, that you may become blameless and harmless, children of God without fault in the midst of a crooked and perverse generation, among whom you shine as lights in the world, holding fast the word of life, so that I may rejoice in the day of Christ that I have not run in vain or labored in vain.
>
> —Philippians 2:14–16

Daily Prayer

Father, reveal Your plan for me today. You have called me to be a representative, a special messenger of Jesus Christ, my Messiah, according to Your will. Help me to be an effective witness, a light shining in the world holding out to others the Word of Life. You have called me to be an agent of prayer, bearing the names of family members, neighbors, friends, and co-workers upon my shoulders as a memorial before You. Thank You for calling me by Your grace and according to Your purpose. Amen.

Day 4

How Big Is Your God?

Daily Scripture Verse

When I consider Your heavens, the work of Your
   fingers,
The moon and the stars, which You have ordained,

What is man that You are mindful of him,
And the son of man that You visit him?

—Psalm 8:4–5

God is the architect and builder of this wondrous universe. He is big enough to measure the waters in the hollow of His hand, to mark off the heavens with a hand span, and enclose the dust of the earth in a measure. He weighed the mountains in scales and the hills in a balance. Yet, He is small enough to live in the heart of a child.

A dad told us about his midnight walk with his son. It was the last night he could keep the promise that they would walk down to the lake before they left to drive home. They were on a trail with trees, underbrush, and snags along the way. The boy was leading the way, confidently chatting away. Suddenly, he turned around, and he couldn't see his dad. His voice became tremulous and high-pitched, "Dad, Dad, where are you?"

Dad walked out from behind a big tree, "Son, I will not leave you alone out here in the dark. There will be times when you won't even sense that God is near, but remember this night. You couldn't see me, but I was nearby, near enough to hear you call."

In a healthy relationship, a child is unafraid when his daddy is near. He can take on the bullies when his daddy is with him. Jesus said that whoever humbles himself like this child is the greatest in the kingdom of heaven. Your heavenly Daddy is always with you; He will never leave or forsake you. No matter the circumstances, God is greater, and all is well. You can take on the bullies of doubt, fear, and unbelief!

Behold, God is my salvation,
I will trust and not be afraid…
He also has become my salvation.

—Isaiah 12:2

*Father, In the name of Jesus, I receive grace and peace,
which You have multiplied to me in the knowledge of
God and of Jesus my Lord. Your divine power has given
to me all things that pertain to life and godliness. Your
grace gives me the ability to fulfill my destiny—walking
in paths You have ordained for me. Your peace directs
me and acts as umpire in all my decisions as I walk with
confidence and assurance. I thank You for giving me the
knowledge of Jesus Christ, who called me by glory and
virtue, and for giving to me exceedingly great and precious promises that through these I may be a partaker of
the divine nature, having escaped the corruption that is
in the world through lust. I live and move and have my
being in Jesus Christ my Lord! Amen.*

Day 5

Keeping First Things First

Daily Scripture Verse

I have this against you, that you have left your first
love.

—REVELATION 2:4

We are living in desperate times. In our ministry we hear
from many family members whose relationships are
fractured. Priorities are out of divine order; career, selfish
ambition, and even ministry sometimes take precedence over
God and family. We forget that healthy relationships with
God, family, and friends are the more important things in life.
Sin, misunderstandings, and unresolved codependency issues

divide and break down our walls of protection. God wants to bring families into a safe dwelling place under the shadow of the Almighty.

Walking circumspectly in our homes and at work is an ongoing learning process. How do I submit to the Holy Spirit's constant ministry of transformation, His promptings reminding me to release resentments, unforgiveness, and bad feelings toward others?

First, I must learn where my responsibility ends and another's begins, quit blaming others for my behavior, and admit my mistakes. I can't change others, but the engrafted Word can save my soul and bring me into emotional wholeness.

Second, I must know who I am in Christ Jesus and live within the boundaries He establishes for me. The Word of God is our guide as we learn to set limits, determining our influence, identification, and integrity.

Third, I must avoid foolish attempts at manipulating others for my own comfort. I must practice speaking, living, and dealing truly.

A person of wisdom makes the most of every opportunity he is given to help develop healthy family relationships and redeem the time lost in selfish, self-centered pursuits. He receives the love of God and gives it away.

> See then that you walk circumspectly, not as fools but as wise, redeeming the time, because the days are evil.
>
> —EPHESIANS 5:15–16

Daily Prayer

> *You are worthy, O Lord, to receive glory, honor, and power, for You have created all things; for Your pleasure*

they are and were created. You predestined me unto the adoption of Your child by Jesus Christ to Yourself, according to the good pleasure of Your will. I pray that my life will always honor and please You as I do good, kind things for others. Amen.

Day 1

More Than a Conqueror

Daily Scripture Verse

In all these things we are more than conquerors through Him who loved us.

—ROMANS 8:37

One of the first things we must do to guard our attitude as a believer is to learn to really believe the truth of Romans 8:37. We are more than conquerors over the world, the flesh, and the devil—but unless we really believe that, we won't act like conquerors.

Jesus said, "In the world you will have tribulation; but be of good cheer, I have overcome the world" (John 16:33). How do you react to problems? Does anxiety overwhelm you? Do you resign yourself to defeat? You can escape defeat by changing your attitude of mind.

At one time negative mind-sets led me to believe that I was a mistake and should never have been born. I believed that bad things happened to me because I was a bad person who could not change. Self-pity dogged my steps, and I looked for someone to rescue me.

But when I really began to believe that because of what Christ had done for me and in me, I had a glorious destiny and future to fulfill, I used spiritual weapons to cast down vain imaginations. Christ freed me from my stinking thinking, and I began to act like the conqueror God had created me to be. You can, too!

For I know the thoughts that I think toward you, says the LORD, thoughts of peace and not of evil, to give you a future and a hope.

—JEREMIAH 29:11

Heavenly Father, because You have turned my captivity and have done great things for me, my mouth is filled with laughter and my tongue with singing. Joy floods my being, and rejoicing covers my lips! The dark clouds of oppression are replaced with Your goodness and its beauty, Father. The cheerfulness of my heart is as medicine to my spirit, soul, and body. It is well with me because I am Yours and You are mine. Your banner over me is love. In the name of Jesus, I rejoice. Amen.

Day 2

Change Your Way of Thinking

Daily Scripture Verse

For as he thinks in his heart, so is he.

—PROVERBS 23:7

*I*n order to guard your attitude as a believer, there will be times when it is necessary to change your thinking. Believing anything begins in the mind. When I was a young girl, my dad told me repeatedly that I could do anything that I made up my mind to do. But I held fast to the misbelief that I was a nonentity without hope for many years. My belief system was flawed and contrary to God's Word until I met the One who loves me with unconditional love.

One of the best ways to begin to change your thinking is to saturate your spirit with the Word of God. After I accepted Christ as my Savior, I began to read the Bible as though God had written it to me personally. I believe that this book is God's love letter to each of His children. Get your Bible out and satu-

rate your spirit with the life-giving truths about how much God loves you and desires for you to be an overcomer. Internalize the Word, and think about it continually. It will help you to guard your attitude from becoming negative. God's thoughts will become your thoughts.

> Finally, brethren, whatever is true, whatever is honorable, whatever is right, whatever is pure, whatever is lovely, whatever is of good repute, if there is any excellence and if anything worthy of praise, dwell on these things.
>
> —PHILIPPIANS 4:8, NASU

Daily Prayer

> *Heavenly Father, You are my light and my salvation. By Your grace, I shall not fear man or become entangled in the ungodly traditions of men. I throw aside every weight and sin that has tried to ensnare me so that I might run the race You have set before me with confidence, efficiency, and effectiveness. I seek to be temperate in all things and run this race to receive a crown of eternal blessedness with certainty. Father, in my life be glorified, in Jesus' name. Amen.*

Day 3

Watch Your Self-Talk

Daily Scripture Verse

> If you abide in Me, and My words abide in you, you will ask what you desire, and it shall be done for you.
>
> —JOHN 15:7

If you want to guard your attitude successfully, not only will you need to think God's Word—you will also need to speak God's Word to yourself. Self-talk will help you to overcome self-defeating thought patterns. When I began to read God's Word to correct my negative thinking, as time slowly went by, and with a lot of scriptural self-talk and prayer, I was able to experience victory over myself. My feelings did not give up easily, but God gave me the strength to persevere. The old attitude of defeat struggled to remain, but I made a decision to believe what God said about me. In spite of the difficulty, I am more than a conqueror through Him!

Early in my walk with God, I thought that He would do everything; He would rescue me and be responsible for my feelings and make life easy. Reading the Bible I realized that God had given us a book of instructions for living the more abundant life.

God expects His children to grow up and take responsibility for their thought patterns and behavior. He gives us the freedom to choose, and He helps us rid our minds of old, unhappy mind-sets. We have a heavenly Father who can be trusted, who will never leave us without support.

I've often heard people say, "It's not whether you win or lose, it's how you play the game." If you play the game of life according to the Word, you'll win! God wants His children to live constructive, victorious lives. God wants us, as believers, to have confidence in His Word, to believe Him rather than our negative belief system.

For the law of the Spirit of life in Christ Jesus has made me free from the law of sin and death.

—ROMANS 8:2

Heavenly Father, I bind my mind to the mind of Christ, my will to the will of God, and my emotions to the control of the Holy Spirit. I choose to walk according to the Spirit of life in Christ Jesus, setting my mind on the things of the Spirit. To be spiritually minded is life and peace. I count myself dead to sin but alive to God in Christ Jesus. Amen.

Day 4

Change Negative Thinking to Positive

Daily Scripture Verse

Strip yourselves of your former nature [put off and discard your old unrenewed self] which characterized your previous manner of life...and be constantly re-newed in the spirit of your mind [having a fresh men-tal and spiritual attitude], and put on the new nature.

—EPHESIANS 4:22–24, AMP

*H*ow can we develop and maintain a winning attitude? We have to totally change our way of thinking from nega-tive to positive. You can do all things through Christ Jesus who strengthens you!

You can change your attitude—let go of past failures, doubt, and unbelief, and go forth as a conqueror in the face of apparent defeat. It appeared that the three Hebrew young men had lost when the king had them thrown into the fiery furnace, but the defeat turned to victory. The crucifixion of Jesus appeared to be a colossal defeat, but this apparent defeat proved to be our victory!

You can take charge of your thoughts, turn doom and gloom into joy and peace, "turn storm clouds into chariots of victory." Every God-begotten person is intended to conquer the world's ways. The conquering power that brings the world to its knees is our faith. The person who wins out over the world's ways is simply the one who believes Jesus is the Son of God. If God be for you, who can be against you?

Change negative feelings to positive. You are who God says you are, more than a conqueror. He created you to win!

> For whatever is born of God overcomes the world. And this is the victory that has overcome the world—our faith. Who is he who overcomes the world, but he who believes that Jesus is the Son of God?
>
> —1 John 5:4–5

Daily Prayer

O Lord, You are my God; I will exalt You, I will praise Your name, for You have done wonderful things, even purposes planned of old [and fulfilled] in faithfulness and truth. Father, You so loved the world that You sent Your only begotten Son to take away our sins. Jesus, I turn to You in every situation for You are my wonderful Counselor, mighty God, everlasting Father, and Prince of Peace. I bind my emotions to the control of the Holy Spirit and my thoughts to the wisdom of God. I renounce old, unpleasant memories that exalt themselves above the knowledge of God and choose to bring them into obedience to the royal law of love. Prince of Peace, I pray that You will be glorified in my public and private life and in my relationships, in the name of Jesus. Amen.

Day 5

Develop an Attitude of Gratitude

Daily Scripture Verse

> But thanks be to God, who gives us the victory through our Lord Jesus Christ.
>
> —1 Corinthians 15:57

*D*evelop an attitude of gratitude and give thanks. There is no better way to guard your attitude than to have an attitude of gratitude. It's hard to have negative thoughts when you are giving thanks!

Uproot worry, fretting, and complaining by shaping your worries into prayer. God will give you peace in the midst of tribulation. Jesus withstood temptation. He has already overcome trials and tribulations, and so can you! As a born-again believer, you have a right to be a winner, to overcome every aspect of this evil world. Think on things that are lovely and loveable, things that are of a good report. Meditate on the Word of God. Begin developing a winning attitude today.

Proclaim: I am more than a conqueror through Him who loves me!

> Giving thanks always for all things unto God and the Father in the name of our Lord Jesus Christ.
>
> —Ephesians 5:20, kjv

Daily Prayer

> *Most Holy God, thank You! Everything in me says, "Thank You!" Thank You for Your love; thank You for Your faithfulness. Most holy is Your name; most holy is Your Word. The moment I called out, You stepped in,*

and You made my life large with strength. You began a good work in me, and I thank You for helping me grow in grace until Your task within me is finally finished on that day when Jesus Christ returns. Your Word equips me for every good work—to do good to everyone, in the name of Jesus. Amen.

Day 1

God Meets Us Where We Are

Daily Scripture Verse

> For you were once darkness, but now you are light in
> the Lord. Walk as children of light.
>
> —EPHESIANS 5:8

On a cold, windy morning I awoke before daylight—my favorite time to meet with my heavenly Father. Through the bedroom door I could see that the great room was flooded with streams of beautiful, soft light. The skylights were open to the light of a full moon suspended from the star-studded sky. Darkness could not absorb or overpower the light.

Once we were darkness; now we are children of the light. Prayer is the key that opens the skylight of our souls to the light of God's love—the genuine, perfect, steadfast light that illumines every person.

This light appeared in my kitchen on a gray, overcast day many years ago. Our three older children were in school, and the baby was asleep in her crib. Sitting at our breakfast table, I was overburdened with the depression that had haunted me since I was six years old, and I no longer wanted to live. Besides feeling that I was a mistake, I had failed as a wife and mother, and I knew that my mood swings were hurting my children. Reasoning that my children would have a better chance to develop into mature individuals if I were no longer a part of their lives, I considered my options.

God meets us where we are. Out of my despair, I called out to an unseen God asking Him to help me. Suddenly a great light came into the room; radiant beams focused on the very spot where I sat. The yellow walls vibrated with life; everything appeared new.

The world inside and outside my window was bathed in purity. My mind cleared, and I was fathoming knowledge beyond my consciousness. Answers to hidden, tormenting questions surfaced, and I understood—before I called, He answered.

My kitchen disappeared, and a field of hardened, brown, crusty fallow ground stretched out across a brilliant, endless space. Gazing upon the landscape, I saw that life was much more than I had ever known existed. Continuing to see with the eyes of my understanding flooded with light, I watched the Holy Spirit turning over the fallow ground of my heart, and underneath was moist, fertile soil for the planting of the Word of God.

> Sow for yourselves righteousness;
> Reap in mercy;
> Break up your fallow ground,
> For it is time to seek the LORD,
> Till He comes and rains righteousness on you.
> —HOSEA 10:12

Daily Prayer

Lord, my trust is in You, and I am unmoved by any circumstance. As the mountains surround Jerusalem, so You surround Your people both now and forevermore. In the name of Jesus I consider it pure joy whenever I face trials of many kinds, because I know that the testing of my faith develops perseverance. Perseverance must finish its work so that I may be mature and complete, not lacking anything. Amen.

Day 2

God Invades Our Desert Places

Daily Scripture Verse

> Behold, I will do something new,
> Now it will spring forth;
> Will you not be aware of it?
> I will even make a roadway in the wilderness
> Rivers in the desert....
> To give drink to My chosen people.
> The people whom I have formed for Myself...
> —ISAIAH 43:19–21, NASU

The harshness of a desert place motivates Christian believers to cry out for deliverance, and our loving Father responds to the cries of His children. Prayer unlocks living waters to flow out into the desert places of negative thinking, resentment, fear, unforgiveness, frustration, doubt, and unbelief.

Even though I grew up in a minister's home, for many years my life was spiritually barren. Seeking fulfillment, I traveled through many desert places until I met the Master—the source of living water. The water He gives is a spring of water welling up to eternal life (John 4:14). I drank freely from God's Word, and He began cleansing me with the washing of water by the Word. My prayers were no longer like clouds without water. A new day had dawned, and change began to take place in our home.

Parenting four children was the most difficult job of my entire life, and my frustrations often led me into a wasteland of guilt, self-doubt, and anxiety. One day, our two older children were having their usual screaming match and chasing each other

with raised fists. As was my custom I took a deep breath to out-shout them, when I stopped, silently asking the Holy Spirit to help me. He gently whispered, "A soft answer turns away wrath." Walking into the room I began speaking to them in a gentle, kind voice. To this day I can see the astonished expressions on their faces as they listened to me. Anxiety moved out as a river of peace flowed from the throne of God.

> He who believes in Me, as the Scripture has said, out of his heart will flow rivers of living water.
>
> —John 7:38

Daily Prayer

> *Father, I bow before You. When I am in a desert place, You will cause streams to spring up and satisfy my thirsty soul. With the help of my comforter, the Holy Spirit, I let go of the past—the mistakes, hurts, and disappointments. I look forward to each new day. You are doing a new thing in my life and in my relationships! In the name of Jesus, I pray. Amen.*

Day 3

A Day of Victory Over Depression

Daily Scripture Verse

> The Lord has anointed me...
> To comfort all who mourn...
> To give them beauty for ashes,
> The oil of joy for mourning,
> The garment of praise for the spirit of heaviness.
>
> —Isaiah 61:1–3

$\mathcal{J}$t was one of those days when long-standing family con-flicts from past and present generations weighed me down. Shadows of memories played hopscotch in my head, and my morning devotions seemed futile. Darkness overwhelmed me, and I wondered how I lost my way to the Father. Laying my Bible and journal aside I sought the Lord.

"O Lord, my God, my Father, I want to come home to Your presence where there is fullness of joy and pleasures forevermore. I am tired of being tired and feeling this awful weight. Reveal the root source of this depression, this anger turned inward."

Opening my Bible I waited for the Lord to answer me. His Word is life and energy. His Word separates the soul and spirit, sifts and exposes the thoughts and intents of the heart. I waited patiently for the Lord, and He heard me.

The answer came: "Rejoice in the Lord always. Again I will say, rejoice" (Phil. 4:4). By faith I began to praise God and offer up thanksgiving for the wonderful things He has done. God inhabits the praises of His people, and praise drives away the shadows of depression. Struggling into my cloak of praise, the spirit of heaviness melted away, dissolving the works of the devil. I found His Word, and the joy of the Lord once again became my strength.

> Your words were found, and I ate them,
> And Your word was to me the joy and rejoicing of my
>   heart;
> For I am called by Your name,
> O Lord God of hosts.
>
> —Jeremiah 15:16

Daily Prayer

> *Lord Jesus, You are a high priest who is touched with the feeling of my infirmities. You were in all points tempted*

as I am; yet You were without sin. You were despised
and rejected of men, a man of sorrows, and acquainted
with grief. I hid as it were my face from You; You were
despised, and I esteemed You not. Forgive me and cleanse
me from all unrighteousness. I am coming boldly unto the
throne of grace, that I may obtain mercy, and find grace
to help in time of need. I thank You for helping me overcome this horrible sense of depression!

Day 4

A Prayer of Desperation

Daily Scripture Verse

> Thus says the LORD, your Redeemer,
> The Holy One of Israel:
> "I am the LORD your God,
> Who teaches you to profit,
> Who leads you by the way you should go."
>
> —ISAIAH 48:17

*F*eeling alone, I stood with the others attending the seminar
as we sang, "God is good all the time. All the time God is
good." The thoughts running around in my head wouldn't settle
down, and the singing did not quiet them.

Silently, I talked to my heavenly Father. "God, I believe that
You are a good God. All these years You have been my life, Your
Word my rod and my staff, but where is my passion for reading
and studying Your love letter to me—the Bible? Where did my
first love go?

"Here I am sitting on the backside of the desert again! How
long will I remain in hibernation? Two years plus is a long time—

even my spirit has gone into hiding. When I read the Word, my eyes jump around from one scripture to another. My purpose in life lies dormant, and I am unproductive. Here I am at another meeting feeling cut off, but my Father, I am looking to You for answers. Why has reading my Bible become laborious?

"Lord, I feel like an exploding Roman candle that has fizzled out. My prayers are like clouds without water. Where are the rivers of living waters that have fed me and kept me energized? Help me, my Lord and my God. Where is it written that I have to take a giant step backwards? Lead me in the way that I am to go."

Adjusting my thinking I began to praise the One who is the lover of my soul. Regardless of my feelings, I will live by faith…I will not draw back unto perdition, but I believe to the saving of my soul.

> It is good that a man should both hope and quietly wait for the salvation of the Lord.
>
> —Lamentations 3:26, kjv

Daily Prayer

Father, today fear is lurking in the shadows. I resist the spirit of fear, for it is written in Your Word again and again, "Fear not. Be not afraid. Let not your heart be troubled." You are my refuge and high tower. You are a refuge and my stronghold in these times of trouble. Thank You for hiding us (my nation, my family, and me) in Your shelter. You have set us high upon a rock, and now shall our heads be lifted up above our enemies round about us. We sing praises to You, O Lord; have mercy and be gracious to us and answer this prayer. Amen.[11]

Day 5

Overcoming the Guilt of Divorce

Daily Scripture Verse

> Behold I will do a new thing,
> Now it shall spring forth;
> Shall you not know it?
> I will even make a road in the wilderness
> And rivers in the desert.
>
> —Isaiah 43:19

Sandy was conscientious and worked diligently at her job. We talked often when I saw her, and it wasn't long before I recognized the hurt, stress, and great inner turmoil and conflict. Some days were worse than others, and I did the only thing I could do: I prayed.

One day when I walked in she was in tears. I gave her a big hug and told her that I was praying for her, and she thanked me. A few weeks later I noticed a change in her—she was laughing and more relaxed than I had ever seen her. When I asked her about the change in her appearance and demeanor, she told me she had gotten divorced.

Sandy had prayed for her husband for years, believing that he would change. With each move across the country, he vowed to quit drinking, he promised to change. As the years went by, the problem worsened. She shared, "The prayers I was praying were not working. It came to me I couldn't change him, and I needed to pray differently."

Sandy asked God to direct her—tell her what to do and give her the courage to do what was best for her children and

herself. God did, and she followed through. You must remember, God knows the end from the beginning.

God has called us to peace, not to a life of confusion and turmoil. God hates divorce, and so do I. Many women who call our offices are asking us to pray for their husbands to be delivered from substance abuse, from the other woman. They want their husbands back home, believing that this time it will different. They want God to change their husbands—to make him quit drinking, doing drugs, and running around with other women.

You can't change your spouse, but you can develop an intimate relationship with God, and He will direct your path. It may be that God is waiting on you to hear from heaven, and He will give you the courage to make the decision that is best for you and your children. Our Father in heaven knows best.

> When you pass through the waters, I will be with you;
> And through the rivers, they shall not overflow you.
> When you walk through the fire, you shall not be
>   burned,
> Nor shall the flame scorch you.
> For I am the LORD your God.
>
> —ISAIAH 43:2–3

Daily Prayer

> *Thank You for releasing me from guilt and shame. I am in Christ Jesus, walking not after the flesh, but after the Spirit, and I am no longer under condemnation. I am blessed; my iniquities are forgiven, and my sins covered. The Lord is not bringing any charge against me. You are not counting my sin against me, and in my spirit is no deceit. Thank You for giving me the grace to accept and forgive myself, for I am wonderfully made. In the name of Jesus, You are my Creator. Amen.*

Day 1

One Starry Night

Daily Scripture Verse

> With my soul I have desired You in the night,
> Yes, by my spirit within me I will seek You early.
>
> —Isaiah 26:9

It was the middle of the night, but I couldn't sleep. I walked into the moonlit great room, and looking up through the skylights I silently prayed, "O God, how long must I wait for an answer?" Family conflicts, my husband's retirement, the cares of the ministry, and my physical health were concerns that had grown to hurricane proportions.

My mind needed quietness, my body rest, and my emotions stillness. Opening the door, I walked outside, and when I looked out across the calm waters, the world became my mirror. The adrenaline that had been flowing for days slowed to a trickle, and I turned my thoughts toward God—the God who never forsakes us…the God who remains faithful even when we aren't.

The storm raging in my soul was stilled. I moved away from the bad memories—the many *little* worries that were spoiling my peaceful garden. There in the stillness of the night I slowed the beating of my heart over personal and ministry concerns. Placing the storm of my troubles on God's altar of everyday trials, I waited to see what would happen. Here in this place of *rest* the Lord appeared to me, and all was well. In the quietness of the moment I could almost feel the brush of His garment as He stood beside me. I traded my tormenting thoughts for quietness; I traded my heavy burdens for His.

The twinkling stars danced on the water, and my soul found solace...my peace passed all understanding.

> For in the day of trouble He will conceal me in His
>   tabernacle;
> In the secret place of His tent He will hide me;
> He will lift me up on a rock.

—Psalm 27:5, nasu

Daily Prayer

Father, I thank You for giving me the grace to believe in You and Your Word even in the midst of the storms of life, providing a place of rest for me. In the midst of seemingly impossible demands, deadlines, and tasks at hand, my heart is steadfast, fixed, trusting in You. Your strength and boldness are released to me as I confidently rest in Your promises. In Your presence I am refreshed, restored, and renewed, in Jesus' name. Amen.

Day 2

Casting Your Care

Daily Scripture Verse

> Cast your burden on the LORD,
> And He shall sustain you;
> He shall never permit the righteous to be moved.

—Psalm 55:22

Wanting to shut out the pain of estrangement, I picked up the new mystery that a friend had loaned to me. My Bible was within reach of the chair where I sat, but I didn't even want to open it. The last time I attempted to read, thoughts

raced through the pathways of my mind like stampeded horses on an open prairie. So I yielded to the voice that beckoned me and began to read. It wasn't long before I was transported to a place far removed from the painful family situation. Completing the book, the heavy burden settled over me as a sodden woolen blanket; I couldn't sleep.

The cares of the past few days piled up, and the mountain of self-blame rose to Alpine heights. There was no way of escape. I was certain that I couldn't scale the mammoth granite blocking the way to the Father.

How was it possible to move this mountain that was menacing and mocking me? Opening my Bible I turned to 1 Peter 5:7: "Casting all your care upon Him, for He cares for you." Placing each family branch in the palms of my hands, I slowly lifted my hands toward the Father. As I began calling each one by name, committing them to the Master, the mountain of fear and anxiety became a molehill. "I'm not taking this care any longer," I asserted. "I've cast them all over there. My children are disciples taught of the Lord. I am an overcomer by the blood of the Lamb and the word of my testimony." As I did, the heavy blanket fell off, and I sang a new song to the Lord.

> Uphold me according to Your word, that I may live;
> And do not let me be ashamed of my hope.
> Hold me up, and I shall be safe.
> —Psalm 119:116–117

Daily Prayer

> *When I call, give me answers. God, take my side! Once, in a tight place, You gave me room; now I'm in trouble again—grace me! Hear me! In my anger I will not sin. When I'm on my bed, I will search my heart and be silent. My trust is in You, Jehovah, my Lord.*

Let the light of Your face shine upon me. Thank You for filling my heart with great joy. I will lie down and sleep in peace, for You alone, O Lord, make me dwell in safety. Amen.

Day 3

Grace in Time of Need

Daily Scripture Verse

Blessed be the God and Father of our Lord Jesus Christ, the Father of mercies and God of all comfort, who comforts us in all our affliction so that we will be able to comfort those who are in any affliction with the comfort with which we ourselves are comforted by God.

—2 Corinthians 1:3–4, nasu

The grandmother's pain was evident in her letter. Would God's grace prove to be more than enough in this situation?

She wrote: "Help! My granddaughter is pregnant. Yesterday just the two of us went out to lunch to celebrate her sixteenth birthday. We got into a heated discussion about her sexual misconduct and her plans to keep the baby.

"Years ago I determined that walking in unconditional love would be my great quest in life. This morning I am writing to you requesting prayer. I feel like the biggest hypocrite walking the earth, and my self-righteousness is sickening. How do I walk in love with this child? How do I forgive her parents who failed to teach her right from wrong? Forgive me, O God; I give up. Change me and give me the grace to walk in love."

Running to the Father, this mother and grandmother asked God to forgive her for condemning and judging her granddaughter. The Father wrapped His arms around her and soothed her heartache. The God of all comfort comforted her, and her granddaughter's behavior was no longer about what this had done to her. She rejoiced, realizing that the power of Christ was resting upon her for good and the good of her family. God's grace moved her into the center of His love—unconditional love that she could give away to her family.

> And He said to me, "My grace is sufficient for you, for My strength is made perfect in weakness."
>
> —2 CORINTHIANS 12:9

Daily Prayer

Father, I thank You for times of refreshing—for hope that arises out of ashes. Faith in God springs up anew, and our faith is spoken of throughout the whole world. Even though some do not believe, their unbelief does not make the faith of God without effect. Let us love one another, for love is of God, and everyone that loves is born of God and knows God. Now abides faith, hope, and love, these three; but the greatest of these is love. We stand shoulder to shoulder in orderly array against the forces of darkness, in the name of Jesus. Amen.

Day 4

My Best Friend

Daily Scripture Verse

There is a friend who sticks closer than a brother.

—PROVERBS 18:24

*W*ords of an old Pentecostal hymn were going round and round in my head like wheels on a bus. "Needing a friend to save me in the end, Where could I go but to the Lord?"[12] Through the passages of time, we often find ourselves in situations where our very best friends can't help us. They may sympathize with us and even offer suggestions, but they can't change the circumstances. We need a friend who will stick closer than a brother or sister; we need supernatural intervention. Where do we go?

Our teenage son's girlfriend was pregnant, and she withstood her mother's urging to have an abortion. After the telephone call, I walked to a place where I could be alone and asked the Holy Spirit to show me what to do. Sensing a need to separate myself for a time alone with God, I called my close friends to let them know that I would not be available for the next few weeks.

Over the next three months I stayed at home, going out only when necessary to run errands or take the children to their after-school activities. At the end of three months, God spoke to me, "Where there is no way, Jesus is the Way," and I was comforted.

Jesus, who is my best friend, is life, and this life is the light of men. I could trust Him with our first grandchild regardless of the circumstances surrounding his birth. Jesus, my best friend would be the light to show him the way to the Father.

> I'm no longer calling you servants because servants don't understand what their master is thinking and planning. No, I've named you friends because I've let you in on everything I've heard from the Father.
> —John 15:15, The Message

The Lord Himself goes before me and will be with me;
He will never leave me or forsake me. I will not be afraid;
I will not be discouraged. O Lord, when I am afflicted,
You hear my desire. You encourage me and listen to my
cry. I am strengthened and encouraged by the Holy Spirit,
and I am encouraged to remain true to the Lord with all
my heart. Amen.

Day 5

The Lord, My Shepherd

Daily Scripture Verse

Save Your people,
And bless Your inheritance;
Shepherd them also,
And bear them up forever.

—Psalm 28:9

Obviously, the Shepherd knew my name, but I could never seem to please Him. The other sheep were so irritating, and I was tired of being prodded while walking from one pasture to another. Deciding that I was more intelligent than those who followed the Shepherd without question, I separated myself from the herd. Besides, the grass looked greener on the hillside across the way.

Remembering the words of the feminists and philosophers, I was confident that I could make my own way in this world. I didn't need anyone telling me what to do. Ignoring the faint voice of warning, I skipped along enjoying the pleasures of sin for a season, and then the green grass turned to dust. The mon-

ster of fear arose, everything around me grew dark, and I didn't know how to go back home. Somewhere from deep inside a thought arose, "There is a way that seems right to a man, but its end is the way of death" (Prov. 16:25).

Just as hopelessness moved in, the Good Shepherd appeared—all alone—without the other ninety-nine. I recognized His voice, and when I looked into His eyes I saw no condemnation, only two pools of liquid love. Rejoicing, He sang a love song to me and carried me in His arms to the springs of living water. Forgiveness washed over me, and I was home where I belonged.

> I am the good shepherd; and I know my sheep, and am known by My own.
>
> —JOHN 10:14

Daily Prayer

> *Because the Lord is my shepherd, I have everything I need. True to Your Word, You let me catch my breath and send me in the right direction. Even though I walk through the valley of the shadow of death, I will fear no evil, for You are with me; Your rod and Your staff, they comfort me. Your goodness and unfailing kindness shall be with me all of my life, and afterwards I will live with You forever in Your home. Amen.*

Day 1

"Hold On" — "Let Go!"

Daily Scripture Verse

> Test all things; hold fast what is good. Abstain from every form of evil.
>
> —1 Thessalonians 5:21–22

One summer day there was a knock at the door of the Church of God parsonage where we lived. Opening the door I greeted Elsie, a church member, and invited her in. My mother came walking up the hallway, and before she could utter a word, Elsie exclaimed, "Sister Griffin, I am on a fast and will not eat again until Germaine is baptized in the Holy Ghost!"

Overwhelming fear struck the pit of my stomach, and I wondered what would happen to Elsie if it didn't happen. Negative, distressing thoughts bombarded me all day. That evening my mother, Elsie, and I went to the church where we knelt at the altar.

After a season of intense praying, my knees gave out, and I sat flat down on the floor. My throat was dry, my *glory*s and *hallelujah*s trickled to an occasional croak, and I wanted to go home. Then in the quietness when all hope was gone, Elsie yelled, "Germaine, *hold on.*" From the opposite side, my mother yelled, "Germaine, *let go.*"

Finally, with my hair plastered to my sweaty brow, I laid my head over on the altar in confusion and defeat. Suddenly, a wind began to blow, my head shot up, and my hands were in the air. Hallelujah! I was baptized in the Holy Spirit, and to my great relief Elsie would be free to eat.

Today, I am grateful for this precious saint who obeyed God and held on, not letting go of the horns of the altar until I

surrendered to the Father of Lights. I believe that when we get to heaven, Mrs. Elsie Bell will receive a reward for every person who has been saved, encouraged, and blessed by Word Ministries and the Prayers That Avail Much® family books.[13]

> The night is far spent, the day is at hand. Therefore let us cast off the works of darkness, and let us put on the armor of light.
>
> —ROMANS 13:12

Daily Prayer

> *Father God, You are my habitation. You have commanded Your angels to guard and keep me in all my ways. I have put on the new man created in Christ Jesus. I renounce resentment, unforgiveness, bitterness, envy, and strife. Satan, the father of lies, is a defeated foe. Lord, You have set Your love upon me; You are my protector and my deliverer. Goodness, mercy, and unfailing love shall follow me all the days of my life. Hallelujah!*

Day 2

What to Hold On To

Daily Scripture Verse

> Therefore, my beloved brethren, be steadfast, immovable, always abounding in the work of the Lord, knowing that your labor is not in vain in the Lord.
>
> —1 CORINTHIANS 15:58

There is an amusing story of a young Christian praying to be filled with the Holy Spirit. While on his knees at the altar an older saint yelled in one ear, "Hold on!" At the same

time, another saint in the opposite ear yelled, "Let go!" Finally, overcome by confusion, he simply passed out!

Unfortunately, the church seems to send mixed messages on many occasions. I hope that you can use this rather humorous story to stir you to press further in loving the Father. He does call to "hold on" and to "let go." Our answer should be, "Yes, Lord!"

We can hold on to faith in His Word. The older saints also had a phrase that said, "Hold on to the horns of the altar until you break through." There is a place in prayer that I call the *RIM*. It's those final moments before going through to victory. It is comparable to the last stage of labor before pushing the baby out. Maybe you who are mothers remember it is the most *intense* time of labor. But shortly after, a birth occurs. You must hold on in those last hours, or minutes, or days of agonizing prayer, for it will bring a reward.[14]

> And let us not be weary while doing good, for in due season we shall reap if we do not lose heart.
>
> —GALATIANS 6:9

Daily Prayer

In the name of Jesus, I arm myself with the full armor of God, armor that God has supplied for me—the helmet of salvation, loins girded with truth, feet shod with the preparation of the gospel of peace, the shield of faith, and the sword of the Spirit, which is the Word of God. With God's armor on, I am able to stand up against all the strategies, deceits, and fiery darts of the devil. I am more than a conqueror through Him who loves me. Amen.

Day 3

What to Let Go Of

Daily Scripture Verse

> Stand fast therefore in the liberty by which Christ has made us free, and do not be entangled again with a yoke of bondage.
>
> —GALATIANS 5:1

What shall we let go of? Let's start with unnecessary weights. "Let us lay aside every weight, and the sin which so easily ensnares us, and let us run with endurance the race that is set before us" (Heb. 12:1).

It appears that the instruction to us is to really let go of any distractions, negative influences, and hindrances to our walk with God. Let go of thoughts and mind-sets of doubts, fears, and unbelief.

The easiest way to let go is to develop a desire to draw close to the Lord. What a precious spiritual goal—to move away from emotions and feelings that can be misleading into a divine fellowship with the Lord. You must learn to lean upon the Lord.

My prayer is to have times of letting go and times of holding on. Times of going up higher and times of refreshing![15]

> One thing I have desired of the LORD,
> That will I seek:
> That I may dwell in the house of the LORD
> All the days of my life,
> To behold the beauty of the LORD,
> And to inquire in His temple.
>
> —PSALM 27:4

> *Lord, You are God. You made us, we are the sheep of Your pasture. I enter into Your gates with thanksgiving and into Your courts with praise. I am thankful unto You and bless Your name. Lord, You are good. Your mercy is everlasting, and Your truth endures to all generations— that includes my children and grandchildren and future generations. I go forth this day rejoicing with a joyous spirit and a glad heart in the name of Jesus. Amen.*[16]

Day 4

Visits With God

> Continue earnestly in prayer, being vigilant in it with thanksgiving.
>
> —COLOSSIANS 4:2

he call to prayer is the Father's invitation to visit with Him." When I read this statement in E. W. Kenyon's book *In His Presence*, I realized that prayer has purpose and is not just a form or ritual.[17]

Back when I read that, we were struggling young mothers. My neighbors and I met often, sharing our hopes, frustrations, dreams, and the complexities of life. No one had any answers, only questions. We voiced our opinions and discussed the latest books and philosophies and the feminine mystique. My life was becoming more complex with each passing day.

BUT GOD! One day while I was sitting alone in my kitchen, a bright light appeared. I was wrapped in love that compelled me to open the door of my heart, and Jesus came in and

introduced me to my teacher—the Holy Spirit. My life became the road that God walks.

Since then I have shared with those who will listen how they can know this God who is our Father and longs to become their close, intimate friend. He is touchable—He is moved with the feelings of our infirmities. He is concerned about everything that concerns you, and He has the answers to life's enigmas.

You can develop a friendship and a partnership with the Creator. As you become more intimately acquainted with Him, you will understand the longings of His heart. He is hungry for the companionship of His family, His sons and daughters.

Visits with God are vital to the believer. When you pray, you experience the presence of God, the fullness of His joy, and you receive power to face the day. His visits turn into a lifetime of continual communication. He never leaves you or forsakes you. He is a companion that sticks closer than a brother.

Jesus said, "Watch and pray that you enter not into temptation." Have you been waiting a long time for your prayers to be answered? Have you grown weary and become tempted to give up? Prayer is essential to the life of the believer. Delight yourself in the Lord, and His desires will become yours.

> But you, beloved, building yourselves up on your most
> holy faith, praying in the Holy Spirit, keep yourselves
> in the love of God, looking for the mercy of our Lord
> Jesus Christ unto eternal life.
>
> —Jude 20–21

Daily Prayer

> *Who among the gods is like You, O Lord? Who is like*
> *You—majestic in holiness, awesome in glory, working*
> *wonders? Who has measured the waters in the hollow*
> *of His hand, or with the breadth of His hand marked*

off the heavens? Who has held the dust of the earth in a basket, or weighed the mountains on the scales and the hills in a balance? Your righteousness reaches to the skies, O God, You who have done great things. Who, O God, is like You? Amen.

Day 5

Behold, All Things Become New

Daily Scripture Verse

But God, who is rich in mercy, because of His great love with which He loved us, even when we were dead in trespasses, made us alive together with Christ.

—EPHESIANS 2:4–5

Sitting in her pastor's study she couldn't believe that he wanted to talk about her relationship with Jesus Christ. Obviously, he didn't hear one word she was telling him. Outraged, she stormed out of his office. With tears streaming down her face, she got in her car, furious that her pastor would imply that her answer was in the Bible. Her children had moved away, and now she was on the brink of another divorce. Everything was falling apart! She was not to blame. Self-pity washed over her, and she allowed her emotions to carry her on tumultuous seas.

No one appreciated that she had sacrificed everything for others. She had laid down her life for them. Her mother, all three husbands, children, and even her pastor had failed her. Her life was one big disappointment, and she wondered why she had been born. Hadn't she tried so hard to please each and every one?

Prayers That Avail Much® *for* Daily Living ❦ Germaine Copeland

That night sitting in her den, she cried out for help, not sure that God would even hear her. BUT GOD, who is rich in mercy, flooded her with the warmth of His love and grace. Old things passed away, and she felt like a brand-new person inside. Peace like a river coursed through her, cleansing the wounds. The healing of her crippled emotions had begun. She was brand-new, and this was the beginning of her journey to victory! She was free to take responsibility for herself, see her faults, and ask for forgiveness. Maybe, there was hope for her marriage. But regardless, she had found the One who loved her unconditionally—the One whose grace is sufficient for every need in every situation.

> And the peace of God, which surpasses all understanding, will guard your hearts and minds through Christ Jesus.
>
> —PHILIPPIANS 4:7

Daily Prayer

> *I ask the God of my Lord Jesus Christ, the glorious Father, to give me the Spirit of wisdom and revelation, so that I may know Him better. May the eyes of my heart be enlightened that I may know the hope to which He has called me, the riches of His glorious inheritance in the saints, His incomparably great power for all who believe. And God raised me up with Christ and seated me with Him in the heavenly realms in Christ Jesus, far above all rule and authority, power and dominion, and every title that can be given, not only in the present age but also in the one to come. Amen.*

Day 1
Precept Upon Precept

Daily Scripture Verse

> But the word of the LORD was to them,
> "Precept upon precept, precept upon precept,
> Line upon line, line upon line."
>
> —ISAIAH 28:13

While preparing to probate my dad's will, I was confident that his wishes would be fulfilled. How did I know what he wanted me to do? He had left his last will—an official document that his attorney had written for him. My dad's signature and the signatures of witnesses are on the final page. I didn't have to fumble through wondering what to do or how to do it. Everything was spelled out—line upon line. While he was living he followed the example of our heavenly Father, who also wrote out His will and testament for His children.

As I was praying for you, the Holy Spirit reminded me about the early beginnings of the Prayers That Avail Much® series. That very first one (known by many as "the little yellow book") and the books that have followed are scriptural prayers taken directly from God's will. "Now this is the confidence that we have in Him, that if we ask anything according to His will, He hears us. And if we know that He hears us, whatever we ask, we know that we have the petitions that we have asked of him" (1 John 5:14–15).

How do we know God's will? Men inspired by the Holy Spirit wrote down God's Word so we can understand what He desires for His children. His plan is revealed in a language that we can comprehend. We can know what to do and how to do it right.

We can take our place as the children of God and know Him intimately. I am so thankful for those years when I spent

precious hours with His Word, the Holy Spirit, and my pen and paper. Had I not known God's will for my children, what would have become of us as a family? I shudder to think about it.

> It's in Christ that you, once you heard the truth and believed it (this Message of your salvation), found yourselves home free—signed, sealed, and delivered by the Holy Spirit.
> —EPHESIANS 1:13, THE MESSAGE

Daily Prayer

> *Thank You for sending Your Son, Jesus, who was made unto me wisdom. Confusion is not a part of my life. I resist confusion about Your will for me, and I trust in You, leaning not unto my own understanding. As I acknowledge You in all my ways, You direct my paths. As I grow in grace I am learning to trust in You completely, and You will show me the path of life. Thank You, Father, in Jesus' name. Amen.*

Day 2

Discover God's Secret Things

Daily Scripture Verse

> So then, men ought to regard us as servants of Christ and as those entrusted with the secret things of God.
> —1 CORINTHIANS 4:1, NIV

There are secrets pertaining to life that the Father has stored up for us. Prayer unlocks this treasure chest of revelation knowledge—knowledge that surpasses our natural thought processes. We have a standing invitation to come boldly to the

throne of grace. Knowing who you are in Christ enables you to approach God the Father with confidence.

In His presence, He will reveal secret things that He keeps ready for those who love Him. The Holy Spirit has come to take the things of Jesus and reveal them unto us, to teach us and lead us into all truth. The Holy Spirit searches diligently, exploring and examining everything, even sounding the profound and bottomless things of God, revealing divine counsels and those things hidden and beyond man's scrutiny (1 Cor. 2:9–10, AMP).

A personal problem situation, a bombshell exploding in our home, launched me into a new study. The problem was consuming us, and I asked the Holy Spirit to teach me how to pray about it. We talked with teachers, counselors, psychologists, and psychiatrists, only to discover that there was no human solution to our problem. We needed divine intervention!

Our home became a battle zone over our son's addictions, and the more we talked, the more resistance we encountered. Turning to the last chapter in the Book of Ephesians, I read, "For we do not wrestle against flesh and blood, but against principalities, against powers, against the rulers of the darkness of this age, against spiritual hosts of wickedness in the heavenly places" (Eph. 6:12). Paul's letter to the believers in Christ Jesus at Ephesus launched me into a ministry that has changed the prayer life of people around the world. For more than twenty years, the Prayers That Avail Much˚ series has remained a bestseller on prayer.

My goal was to bring deliverance and salvation to our son. I wanted him to change his behavior, but before I enjoyed the fruit of my prayers for him, the engrafted Word of God brought salvation to my soul—healing emotional wounds, meeting personal needs, and bringing down strongholds, wrong thought patterns that I had exalted above the knowledge of God.

This letter written by Paul is my prayer book and guide

for daily life. When I ask for wisdom, He answers. When I ask about my responsibility as a wife, He answers. When I ask Him to teach me to pray prayers that avail much, He answers. God is faithful and eager to reveal divine secrets to His children.

> In Him…you were sealed with the Holy Spirit of promise, who is the guarantee of our inheritance until the redemption of the purchased possession, to the praise of His glory.
>
> —Ephesians 1:13–14

Daily Prayer

> *Father, You made Jesus to be sin for us, who knew no sin; that we might be made the righteousness of God in Him. My earnest (heartfelt, continued) prayer makes tremendous power available—dynamic in its working. Father, I live in You—abide vitally united to You—and Your words remain in me and continue to live in my heart. I ask whatever I will, and it shall be done for me to Your great glory! Amen.*

Day 3

God Gives the Vision

Daily Scripture Verse

> Where there is no vision, the people perish: but he that keepeth the law, happy is he.
>
> —Proverbs 29:18, KJV

Everyone has a divine destiny. God who created all things according to His will determined your paths, and He imparted special grace, gifts, and talents to you even while you were in your mother's womb. You are created for His pleasure.

A question we often ask ourselves is: "Why am I here?" Until we settle this issue, we often entertain depression and hopelessness. When God gives you the vision, He equips and anoints you to fulfill your destiny. Occasionally, I have met a person who has known since childhood what he wanted to do with his life. He perceives and contemplates with pleasure his future. Life has purpose.

Word Ministries was organized in 1977 when God gave me a vision of the world map. I could see Word Ministries at the center with beams of light shooting forth continually to every part of the globe. I didn't understand its meaning at the time. Now I know that the beams represent each one who is united with us in prayer. We are members one of another, soldiers in the army of the Lord, praying for every tribe, nation, and people!

Yes, it can be overwhelming, but then we remember: "For God so loved the world that He gave His only begotten Son, that whoever believes in Him should not perish but have everlasting life" (John 3:16).

When we pray and stand united in prayer, we are world changers! There is power in agreement; there is power in connection. When we get busy with God's agenda, He will perform Romans 8:28 in our lives, perfecting those things which concern us.

> And we know that all things work together for good to those who love God, to those who are the called according to His purpose.

Daily Prayer

Jesus is Lord, and everything is all right! Your plan is to prosper me and not to harm me. Your plan is to give me hope and a future. Thank You for listening to me when I call upon You, praying to You. I love You because You

first loved me. And I know that in all things, God works
for the good of those who love Him, who have been called
according to His purpose. Even in the face of adversity I
declare, "All is well." Amen.

Day 4

The Road God Walks

Daily Scripture Verse

Your word is a lamp to my feet
And a light to my path.

—Psalm 119:105

I do not remember where I first read these words: "My life is the road God walks." It seemed that suddenly they were emblazoned on the portals of my mind and on my heart. In retrospect, I see the narrative of my life portrayed on God's eternal landscape, and my life is interconnected with people from past, present, and future generations.

Each life is an eternal highway, never ending, but always leading either to a brighter day or on into the darkness. Viewing this canvas, I recognize unlit roads with many obstacles waiting for the light. Other pathways are rocky with detours. Here and there is a glimmer of light, and occasionally there appears a road that emanates radiant beams of glorious light. All along each roadway are signposts pointing to life eternal.

Standing at a distance, I observe the roadway of life I had walked. I observe the familiar, dark, dead-end street where I was a nonentity. There were many "arteries" that exited my road, and more often than not I ended up at Frustration Village, and there was no way out. I had to return the way I had come.

That was my life—I was trapped, restless, and yearning, yet I always knew that somewhere there had to be joy and peace.

On the most memorable day of my life, light finally broke through, and the road—my life—was lit with a brilliancy that exceeds description. And not only were my eyes flooded with light, but I was also absorbed by the light—my entire being became light.

Many voices call out at the exit signs, but I follow the light that becomes brighter and brighter. The road God walks is filled with righteousness, peace, love, and joy. Jesus is the Lord, the Master of my life. Traveling this road is an adventure, sometimes painful, but always there is peace and joy. There's a song in my heart, and it's the rhythm that I walk to—He orders my steps in His Word![18]

> Order my steps in thy word: and let not any iniquity have dominion over me.
>
> —Psalm 119:133, KJV

Daily Prayer

> *Father, may I always listen for Your gentle whisper. Thank You for sending the Holy Spirit to take me by the hand and guide me into all the truth. He speaks only what He hears, and He will tell me what is yet to come. In all my ways I acknowledge You, and You shall direct my path. In the name of Jesus, I thank You for Your great love for me. Amen.*

Day 5

Knowing the Will of God

Daily Scripture Verse

> And do not be conformed to this world, but be transformed by the renewing of your mind, that you may

prove what is that good and acceptable and perfect
will of God.

—Romans 12:2

*T*he businessman who worked nearby began coming by our offices periodically to ask us to pray. He desperately wanted to know God's will for his life. Unlike many Christians who struggle with this, he did find the path he was to follow, which required some big changes in his life, including a move and cut in salary.

The Father has destined and appointed His children to come progressively to know His will. Bill continued going to church, worked diligently at his career, asked faithful intercessors to pray for him to know the will of God, and studied and meditated on the Scriptures. He didn't just sit down—but worked at what his hand found to do. As Bill worked, God worked to fulfill His promise in Philippians 2:13: He was "all the while effectually at work in you [energizing and creating in you the power and desire], both to will and to work for His good pleasure and satisfaction and delight" (AMP).

Our youngest daughter, who is a woman of many talents, loves God with all that is within her. Lynn's life had not gone as she had planned, and now she prayed to know what God would have her do—she wanted to know His will for her life. Like Bill, she read her Bible, prayed diligently, and worked diligently. Her desire to have an intimate relationship with her heavenly Father called her to the prayer closet each morning.

Realizing that her education and training experience were not to be wasted, she felt guilty about not doing enough in her church and community. But God was at work, revealing His good, acceptable, and perfect will for her.

The Holy Spirit spoke to her for many months from a scripture that seemed to jump out at her in strange places. "But if anyone does not provide for his own, and especially for those

of his household, he has denied the faith, and is worse than an unbeliever" (1 Tim. 5:8).

Surely, this couldn't be for her. She was doing everything she knew to do for her husband and four young children, so how could this scripture apply to her? While sitting in church one day, this verse popped out again. In this atmosphere of worship, the Holy Spirit began to talk to her: "Do not sacrifice your family for good works. Your ministry at this present time is to make disciples of your children and to teach them to obey everything I have commanded you. I am with you."

There are times when she has opportunities to share in small groups the revelations that God is giving her, but her ministry at home is her priority.

> Roll your works upon the Lord [commit and trust them wholly to Him; He will cause your thoughts to become agreeable to His will, and] so shall your plans be established and succeed.
>
> —PROVERBS 16:3, AMP

Daily Prayer

Thank You for sending Your Son, Jesus, who was made unto me wisdom. I resist confusion about Your will for me, and trust in You, leaning not unto my own understanding. As I acknowledge You in all my ways, You direct my paths. Growing in grace I am learning to trust in You completely, and You will show me the path of life. Confusion is far from me. Thank You, Father, in Jesus' name. Amen.

Day 1

The Power of Praise

Daily Scripture Verse

"Do you hear what these children are saying?" they asked him. "Yes," replied Jesus, "have you never read, 'From the lips of children and infants you have ordained praise'?"

—MATTHEW 21:16, NIV

God's mighty weapons are available to us. Prayer, faith, hope, love, praise, God's Word, the Holy Spirit—these are powerful and effective weapons. One of the most powerful weapons or spiritual tools is praise.

What is praise? Praise eulogizes God, conveying the idea of boastful singing or speaking about His glorious virtues and honor. Speak well of our Father, tell of His goodness, adore Him, and give Him an audible celebration. Quiet or boisterous praise will still and silence the enemy. God inhabits the praises of His people

It takes determination to praise the Lord. Offer thanksgiving in celebration of God, who He is, and what He does. You are ushered into God's presence on the wings of praise. Sincere and honest praise releases God's sovereignty and power into human circumstances.

Praise will overthrow satanic captivity! Joyful praise opens prison doors, preparing the way of salvation (Acts 16:25–26). Praise repels and replaces the spirit of heaviness (Isa. 61:3). Praise releases power and the anointing that destroys yokes and moves burdens (Matt. 21:16).

Joyful praise releases blessings and satisfaction. His unfailing love is better than life itself; praise Him! Honor Him. Lift up your hands to Him in prayer. He will satisfy you more than

the richest of foods. Praise Him with songs of joy. Praise will release rivers of living water, washing away anxiety, fear, and depression. Praise stops the advancement of wickedness and drives out the temptations to sin (Ps. 7:14–17).

Praise is for all seasons. Don't wait until all your circumstances are favorable. Bless the Lord at all times; let His praises be continual in your mouth! And when you find yourself in seasons of trials or temptation, praise Him!

> We are human, but we don't wage war with human plans and methods. We use God's mighty weapons, not mere worldly weapons, to knock down the Devil's strongholds. With these weapons we break down every proud argument that keeps people from knowing God. With these weapons we conquer their rebellious ideas, and we teach them to obey Christ.
>
> —2 Corinthians 10:3–5, nlt

Daily Prayer

> *Father, You are worthy of all praise. We praise You for Your mighty acts, according to Your excellent greatness. We will praise You in the sanctuary with instruments and with the dance; with stringed instruments and organs; with cymbals and high-sounding cymbals. As long as we have breath, we will praise You, Father God, in the holy name of Jesus. You are a mighty God! Hallelujah!*

Day 2

The Power of a Smile

Daily Scripture Verse

Thou hast made known to me the ways of life; thou

shalt make me full of joy with thy countenance.

*D*o you really believe that God is God, and what He does for others He will do for you? Your countenance speaks volumes. Several years ago, my family and I were visiting my parents. On Sunday morning along, with other family members, we attended church where my father, Rev. A. H. "Buck" Griffin, served as pastor. The choir sang in harmony, "It is joy unspeakable and full of glory. Oh, the half has never yet been told."

That afternoon while we were sitting at the lunch table talking and laughing, my brother who was home on furlough said, "The choir members need to notify their faces of the joy they sang about today." They loved the Lord and were intense in their praises, and I understood.

Even though smiling had become natural, I was always very intense in my praise and worship, never thinking about my expression. But this changed when I attended a Christian concert, where it seemed the ceiling above my head disappeared and I saw Jesus. He was smiling at me! On impulse I smiled back—the muscles in my back, neck, and face relaxed, and my frown automatically disappeared. Jesus said, "My people screw up their faces, thinking that they are proving their sincerity. They try so hard to worship Me in spirit and truth, but are too uptight to hear My laughter. I rejoice over you with singing— with a joyful countenance. I am here to show you the path of life. In My presence is fullness of joy; at My right hand are pleasures forevermore."

The Father is your exceeding great joy; He is the health of your countenance! Fellowship with Him and smiling will become natural and genuine. Your happy heart is good medicine, and your cheerful mind works healing. The light in your

eyes rejoices the hearts of others. Your countenance will radiate the joy of the Lord.

It has been said that smiling costs nothing but creates much good. It enriches those who receive it without impoverishing those who give it away. It happens in a flash, but the memory of it can last forever. No one is so rich that he can get along without it. No one is too poor to feel rich when receiving it. It creates happiness in the home, fosters good will in business, and is the countersign of friends. It is rest to the weary, daylight to the discouraged, sunshine to the sad, and nature's best antidote for trouble. Yet it cannot be bought, begged, borrowed, or stolen, for it is something of no earthly good to anybody until it is given away willingly.

> Delight yourself [smile] also in the LORD,
> And He shall give you the desires of your heart.
> —PSALM 37:4

Daily Prayer

Where the Spirit of the Lord is, there is liberty—emancipation from bondage, freedom. Father, I praise You with joyful lips because I am ever filled and stimulated with the Holy Spirit. I speak out in psalms and hymns, making melody with all my heart to You, my Lord. My happy heart is good medicine, and my cheerful mind works healing. The light in my eyes rejoices the heart of others; my countenance radiates the joy of the Lord. The joy of the Lord is my strength! Amen.

Day 3

Receive Love, and Give Love

Daily Scripture Verse

> And this is His commandment: that we should believe
> on the name of His Son Jesus Christ and love one
> another, as He gave us commandment. Now he who
> keeps His commandments abides in Him, and He in
> him. And by this we know that He abides in us, by the
> Spirit whom He has given us.
>
> —1 JOHN 3:23–24

The six-year-old with the brown hair streaked blonde by the sun reached up to hug her mother goodnight, saying, "Oh Mommy, God loves me when I'm good, and He loves me when I'm bad."

Giving her daughter one last big hug, the mother tucked her in bed. That night, pondering her little girl's insight, she wondered why she did not feel this way. Did God really love her when her performance level was so imperfect? She realized she was uncomfortable in the Father's presence.

Sometimes, God speaks to us out of the mouths of babes. Our work, our responsibility is to believe and to love one another.

Our performance will never merit His love and favor. He proved His love to us when we were yet sinners. Now He waits for you to receive His unconditional love. Yes, especially you! Receive this love of God, and look for someone to give His love to each day.

A smile will speak to the brokenhearted; a calm, gentle spirit will still turbulent waters; a soft answer will turn away wrath; and well-chosen words can heal those who are hurting and looking for

answers. You are a love gift to the world because you are born of love. You can love others because He first loved you. When you are tempted to react negatively to situations, remember the Holy Spirit is present to help you, and your gentle speech will break down rigid defenses. The Lord will make you to increase and abound in love one toward one another and toward all men.

> No one has ever seen God; but if we love one another, God lives in us and his love is made complete in us.
>
> —1 John 4:12, niv

Daily Prayer

> *Father, I eagerly pursue and seek to acquire love (making it my aim and my great quest). Also, I earnestly desire and cultivate the spiritual endowments (gifts). When I was a child, I talked like a child, I thought like a child. Now that I have become a man/woman, I am done with childish ways and put them aside. My desire is to walk in love—true affection for God and man, growing out of God's love for me, in the name of Jesus. Amen.*

Day 4

The Hall of Faith

Daily Scripture Verse

> Now faith is the substance of things hoped for, the evidence of things not seen.
>
> —Hebrews 11:1

Reading chapter 11 of Hebrews is a walk through the Hall of Faith. The Old Testament saints who are mentioned encourage and strengthen us to persevere in faith. In spite of

the ridicule of neighbors, Noah obeyed God and built the ark. Abraham, who was called to go into a new life and a new land, obeyed God, not knowing where he was going. By faith Sarah, together with Abraham, was able to bear a child, even though they were too old and she was barren. Moses tried to talk his way out of obeying, but by faith he led his people out of bondage. Would I have endured as Joseph did? Others are listed, and their obedience and perseverance are an inspiration to me. God is faithful, and faithful is He who calls who will also do it. God gives the vision; our responsibility is to obey.

Recently, a friend sent me an article about a modern-day hero of faith who remains true to his vision. Rev. Billy Graham, a wonderful example to us, is one who has spent his life in obedience and service to the King of kings and the Lord of lords, our Redeemer, Savior, and soon-coming King. We can safely follow him as he follows Jesus, carrying out the Great Commission.

We are all witnesses and have received the power to share Jesus with others. Let us be about the Father's business, telling others about the Savior who came to redeem mankind—to save us from our sins. We are living witnesses to the transforming power of God. Souls are crying for the peace of God that passes all understanding, the love of God that is unconditional.

Pray for your family; pray for your friends, your church, your community, and your country. Pray for your enemies. God hears and answers prayer. Praying will prepare you to minister in love both by word and by your godly lifestyle.

Be faithful until death, and I will give you the crown of life.

—REVELATION 2:10

Daily Prayer

> Jesus is my Lord, and I will not lose heart. Even though
> my outward man is perishing, yet my inward man is being
> renewed day by day. For this light affliction, which is but
> for a moment, is working for me a far more exceeding and
> eternal weight of glory, while I look at the things that are not
> seen. Thank You for the eternal things that will never pass
> away, in the name of Jesus. Amen.

Day 5

Trusting in God

Daily Scripture Verse

> In God I have put my trust;
> I will not be afraid.
> What can man do to me?
>
> —Psalm 56:11

One morning the telephone rang, and when I answered it a distressed grandmother shared the intense worries and irrational fears that had plagued her. When her children were in school, she lived in dread until they returned home in the afternoon. When her husband was out of town, her anxieties intensified; the ringing of the telephone was an ominous sound, and she was afraid to answer and afraid not to. Now her married children were doing well, but she couldn't shake the feeling that something horrible was going to happen. She wanted to know how she could be free of this torment.

At one time I had lived with these same fears. The God of comfort taught me how to overcome irrational fear, and I was able to strengthen and comfort her. I assured her that God was no

respecter of persons, and she believed that what He had done for me He would do for her. Agreeing to frame all her worries with prayers of thanksgiving and praise, she began each morning by making a joyful sound to the Lord, acknowledging that He is God.

In the beginning it wasn't easy, but she proclaimed, "Father God, thank You that my husband and our children and their children dwell in the secret place of the Most High. They shall remain stable and fixed under the shadow of the Almighty, which no foe can withstand." She declared Psalm 91 as a song of praise. Her fears were replaced with faith—*the substance of things hoped for and the evidence of things not seen.* The joy of the Lord became her strength, and fear was defeated, for God had not given her the spirit of fear, but of power, love, and a sound mind (2 Tim. 1:7).

Prayers of affirmation transformed her thinking, and the love of God filled her heart, turning fear out of doors. Praying from God's Word will give you confidence and enable you to approach the Father intelligently, knowing that your prayers will avail much.

> But let all those that put their trust in thee rejoice: let them ever shout for joy, because thou defendest them: let them also that love thy name be joyful in thee.
> —PSALM 5:11, KJV

Daily Prayer

> *Father, I love Your name. I have trusted in Your mercy; my heart rejoices in Your salvation. Thank You, Lord, for watching over my family. You are our defender and Savior. Assign us godliness and integrity as our bodyguards, for I expect You to protect my family and me. Lord, You are my rock, my fortress, and my deliverer; my God, my strength, in whom I will trust; my buckler, the horn of my salvation, and my high tower. Thank You for keeping us safe, in the name of Jesus. Amen.*

Day 1

Enjoying His Presence

Daily Scripture Verse

> You have made known to me the ways of life;
> You will make me full of joy in Your presence.
>
> —ACTS 2:28

One of my daughters enjoyed being with me wherever I was. Bringing her toys with her, she followed me as I moved from room to room taking care of my daily chores. We were both busy, and few words were spoken. Everything was right with her world because she was in my presence. This gave me a glimpse of how to come before the Father as a little child.

The house was quiet, and I had a few quiet moments. Drawing the rocker nearer to the fireplace, I sat with my Bible opened to the Book of Psalms. My eyes skipped from one highlighted verse to another, as I delighted in the presence of my Father. Closing my eyes I said, "Father, I just come to be with You today. You are the Good Shepherd, and I have no need except to know You more intimately. I have come simply because I enjoy being with You."

In His quiet manner the Father spoke, "Germaine, I have supplied all your needs according to My riches in glory."

Pure love poured over my being, and I answered, "Yes, I know, and I am so thankful."

His voice came again: "Did you know that I supply all your emotional needs?"

Sitting silently, meditating on God's spoken word to me, I remained bathed in the warmth of His embrace. I am my Beloved's, and He is mine. His banner over me is love, and everything is all right in my world.

> One thing have I desired of the LORD, that will I seek after; that I may dwell in the house of the LORD all the days of my life, to behold the beauty of the LORD, and to inquire in his temple.
>
> —PSALM 27:4, KJV

Daily Prayer

> *Lord, thanks for this day that You have made. I rejoice, and I am glad in it! I rejoice in You always, and again I say, I rejoice. I delight myself in You, and I am happy because God is my Lord! Thank You for loving me and rejoicing over me with joy. Hallelujah! I am redeemed. I come with singing, and everlasting joy is upon my head. I obtain joy and gladness; sorrow and sighing flee away. I rejoice in God my Savior! Amen.*

Day 2

Enlarge My Heart That I Might Know You More

Daily Scripture Verse

> …that I may know Him and the power of His resurrection, and the fellowship of His sufferings, being conformed to His death.
>
> —PHILIPPIANS 3:10

My heart expands to receive more of the knowledge of God. Daily I cry out, "Oh, that I might know You, my Lord Jesus Christ…that I might know and understand the power of Your resurrection, and the fellowship of Your sufferings. Then I will be made conformable to Your death. Only then can Your resurrection be reflected in my life, my behavior, so that my very existence is a testimony to You."

In the beginning of my walk with God, I voraciously read His Word—I couldn't read enough—I couldn't read fast enough. I didn't dare speed-read for fear that I might miss something. Every word that proceeds from the mouth of God is nourishment to my soul. His words were found, and I did eat them. They are truly the joy and the rejoicing of my heart. Oh, that I might know Him, my Lord, my God, my master, my life.

"There is a name that I love to hear, and I love to sing His praises." If I wasn't speaking His Word, I was singing His Word. :His name is music to my ears—the greatest name on earth. Oh, how I love Jesus." Why? "Because He first loved me. That Name! The power of that Name! The precious ointment poured forth soothing painful memories—healing my body and restoring my soul. "Oh, how I love Jesus!"[19]

Riding through the Great Smoky Mountains my very being overflows with the beauty of the earth. Everywhere I look, rays of sunlight bounce off the golden branches of trees proclaiming the Son of Righteousness who rose with healing in His wings. The vibrant hue of red leaves proclaims life is in the blood that washes away sin. Midst the variegated colors of fall, evergreens proclaim the faithfulness of our God. My soul resounds with shouts of hallelujahs—how great Thou art!

Oh, that I might have mastery of words that I know not yet! Oh, that I might have a thousand tongues. I would praise Your name with unending vocabulary.

I will bow down toward your holy temple
    and will praise your name
    for your love and your faithfulness,
for you have exalted above all things
    your name and your word.

—PSALM 138:2, NIV

> *Father, thank You for loving me! You are holding my right hand! You will keep on guiding me all my life with Your wisdom and counsel, and afterwards receive me into the glories of heaven! For I am convinced that neither death nor life, neither angels nor demons, neither the present nor the future, nor any powers, neither height nor depth, nor anything else in all creation, will be able to separate me from the love of God that is in Christ Jesus our Lord. Amen.*

Day 3

Come Home to the Father

Daily Scripture Verse

> I will dwell in them
> And walk among them.
> I will be their God,
> And they shall be My people.

—2 CORINTHIANS 6:16

While sitting in my kitchen, meditating on life in general, the glory of the Lord shone round about, and more than life itself I wanted to know God. The Holy Spirit became my companion and teacher. He revealed the reality of Jesus to me—and to know Jesus is to know the Father. The Godhead dwelled with me. I am His people!

A lifetime of adventure began immediately. The way to the Father opened up, and through the pages of the Bible I discovered the portrait of my Lord and my God. The Bible was no longer just a history book, no longer a book of poetry, no

longer letters written to ancient people of past empires; the Bible became God's personal love letter to me.

My perception of a stern, rigid, severe God was replaced with the image of a loving, compassionate Father God. This new perception was drawn on the tablets of my heart. I was the prodigal who had come home to a Father who ran to scoop me up in His embrace. Strongholds that had separated me from His love were demolished; it was a new day!

> When he was still a great way off, his father saw him
> and had compassion, and ran, and fell on his neck and
> kissed him.
>
> —LUKE 15:20

Daily Prayer

> I confess with my mouth the Lord Jesus and believe in
> my heart that God has raised Him from the dead—I am
> saved. For with my heart I believe unto righteousness,
> and with my mouth confession is made unto salvation.
> Father, I thank You for redeeming me from the law of sin
> and death. I walk after the Spirit of life in Christ Jesus,
> and I am no longer under condemnation. I have passed
> from death to life! Amen.

Day 4

Transformation

Daily Scripture Verse

> This is the day the LORD has made;
> We will rejoice and be glad in it.
>
> —PSALM 118:24

*E*very morning I turned over and reached for the covers to drown out my father's booming voice, "It's getting-up time! This is the day the Lord has made; rejoice and be glad! Wake up, wake up all over—spirit, soul, and body."

One of the rules when my husband and I were married was that he would not talk to me until I had my morning coffee. This worked for us until our son started school. One morning while standing at the door with my husband and son, I said, "Have a great day!"

Rather than telling me good-bye and hurrying off, my husband held the door open, looked me in the eye, and said very quietly, "How do you expect us to have a good day when you are always so grouchy in the mornings?"

Closing the door in my face, he and our son descended the front steps. Huddled in my bathrobe, I walked to the window and watched as he helped our first-grader in the car. Feeling remorseful, I went to the kitchen and sat down at the table, realizing that I needed an attitude adjustment.

My dad's voice echoed down through the years, "When you wake up, wake up all over—spirit, soul, and body." Could I possibly be punishing my family to get even with my dad? How futile!

Asking God to forgive me for my resentment toward my dad, I made a commitment to myself that I would be happy in the mornings and spread a little cheer to my family. To my surprise, I soon loved rising early before the world was awake (just like my dad), and his advice became a positive force in my life. Little by little changes occur—from glory to glory the Holy Spirit is changing me.

> But we all, with unveiled face, beholding as in a mirror
> the glory of the Lord, are being transformed into the

same image from glory to glory, just as by the Spirit
of the Lord.

—2 CORINTHIANS 3:18

Daily Prayer

*This morning, regardless of circumstances, I choose to
rejoice in the Lord and be glad. The old things of yesterday have passed away, and behold, all things are new.
Because of the Lord's mercies I am not consumed, because
His compassions fail not. They are new every morning:
great is Your faithfulness.*

Day 5

He Came for My Vow

Daily Scripture Verse

When you make a vow to God, do not delay to pay
   it....
Pay what you have vowed—
Better not to vow than to vow and not pay.

—ECCLESIASTES 5:4–5

Attending an annual camp meeting in the summer of 1951,
I wondered what I was supposed to do with my life. My
dreams of going to college had been dashed. The missionary
who was speaking that afternoon caught my attention, and I
found myself listening attentively. Gradually the speaker's voice
faded, and the hundreds of people evaporated, leaving me all
alone in a secret place with God. In that quiet moment, I recognized God's call to me—a call to ministry.

Dismayed, I assumed I would have to be a missionary in far
and distant lands. I felt God must be somehow punishing me,

and I immediately began looking for a way of escape. Scriptures tell us that we perish for a lack of knowledge, and I had no reliable knowledge of God—I didn't know God. My perception of Him was flawed. I saw Him as a cruel, unbending, and demanding Father.

Unaware that God's callings are irrevocable and without repentance, I made my conditional vow. I promised to obey Him if He would allow me to get married and have a family before sending me to the jungles of Africa or India.

At the close of the service I walked the long aisle along with many others and gave God my most prized possession—a watch I had received for my birthday. This noble offering sealed our agreement—an agreement that I soon forgot.

In January of 1968, after the birth of our fourth child, God came for my vow. Stuck in depression, and not even knowing what was wrong, I called upon God to rescue me. Suddenly beams of light drew me into a place of warmth and safety. I sat mesmerized while my fragmented, crippled emotions were sucked up into a beautiful, cosmic kaleidoscope.

The kaleidoscope gave way to a field of hardened, brown, fallow ground stretched out across the spacious brilliancy. Gazing upon the landscape, I watched the Farmer plow the earth as geysers of hot liquid exploded from the depths of my soul. Furrow after furrow yielded moist, fertile soil, and the aroma of newly well-irrigated dirt transported me into the secret place with God. Tears flowed freely as He prepared the ground for the planting of His Word. This I discovered—*God is love!*

The Father has graciously included each of us in His plan of redemption. God loves you, and He will come for your vow at the appropriate time. He is never early, nor is He ever late. He is an awesome God who has foreordained your pathways and called you with a holy calling.

God is faithful, by whom you were called into the fellowship of His Son, Jesus Christ our Lord.

—1 CORINTHIANS 1:9

Daily Prayer

Lord, my God, when I make a vow to You, I will not be slow to pay it. I give You my true thanks and fulfill my promises. Lord, I trust You in times of trouble so You can rescue me, and I will give You glory. When I talk to You, my God, and vow to You that I will do something, I'll not delay in doing it, for You have no pleasure in fools. I keep my promise to You knowing that the Holy Spirit is the keeper at the door of my lips. Amen.

Day 1

Forgive the Past Generation

Daily Scripture Verse

> For He who is mighty has done great things for me,
> And holy is His name.
> And His mercy is on those who fear Him
> From generation to generation.
>
> —LUKE 1:49–50

You are God's representative, and He has placed you in an important position. Whether or not you realize it, you pass on to future generations blessings or curses. How do we pass on these generational blessings that we received from our parents and grandparents? How do curses get passed on even though we have good personal relationships with our Father God?

Much too often we pass along generational curses with our words and behavior. Many fathers and mothers who have unresolved issues from the past declare that they will never be like their parents, only to find themselves displaying attitudes that disappoint and condemn themselves.

The child of God is to be an imitator of the heavenly Father. We imitate those to whom we have given our attention. Are you harboring unforgiveness and resentment toward an earthly parent, rather than giving allegiance and preeminence to the God of your salvation? Let us forgive the past generation their mistakes so that we may be forgiven.

> I call heaven and earth as witnesses today against you, that I have set before you life and death, blessing and cursing; therefore choose life, that both you and your descendants may live.
>
> —DEUTERONOMY 30:19

Abba Father, thank You for sending Jesus who brought us out from under doom by taking the curse for our wrong-doing upon Himself. We have witnessed the fruit of disobedience—the iniquities of the fathers passed down to the present generation. We repent and renounce our sins and the sins of our ancestors, and we ask You to forgive us and cleanse us from all unrighteousness. In the name of Jesus we break generational curses of our earthy fathers and bow ourselves before You, our heavenly Father who is faithful, forgiving, loving, kind, compassionate, and full of mercy. Amen.

Day 2

God's Woman

Daily Scripture Verse

Then God said, "Let Us make man in Our image, according to Our likeness; let them have dominion over the fish of the sea, over the birds of the air, and over the cattle, over all the earth and over every creeping thing that creeps on the earth." So God created man in His own image; in the image of God He created him; male and female He created them.

—GENESIS 1:26–27

*B*efore I began speaking I paused and looked at the congregation of women who had set aside this Saturday for an all-day seminar and luncheon. Women who sat with eyes downcast and heads bowed outnumbered the self-confident, the well-dressed. Most had grown up in church, hearing the same doctrine I had been taught from birth.

Sending up one more silent prayer, I took a deep breath and began. "Ladies, before we can teach and train others we must know who we are and why we were created. Genesis 1:26–27 gives woman equality in dominion with man. God planned for man and woman to have dominion together under His rulership.

"Woman lost her place of authority when she focused all her love on man. She replaced her allegiance to God by placing her utter dependence in man. She made man her lord, and he began to rule over her. This was never God's intention. His desire is to have man and woman living together in harmony and agreement, cooperating with one another."

Fuchsia Pickett wrote, "As God delivers His church from the bondage of tradition and culture—and from fallen man's doctrine of divine order—we will see man and woman function together to build godly homes and to fulfill God's purpose for the building of His kingdom. When redemption cleanses us from the desire to rule, man and woman will not be threatened by each other, but will welcome each other's godly counsel. This is the hour."[20]

> There is neither Jew nor Greek, there is neither slave nor free, there is neither male nor female; for you are all one in Christ Jesus.
>
> —GALATIANS 3:28

Daily Prayer

Father, I thank You for regarding me as Your special treasure. Keep me as the apple of Your eye. You cause me to be a woman of noble character. Lead me in the way I should go, and with the Holy Spirit as my Helper, I will do great exploits for Your kingdom, in the name of Jesus. Amen.

Day 3

What Is Love, Anyway?

Daily Scripture Verse

> By this we know love, because He laid down His life
> for us. And we also ought to lay down our lives for the
> brethren.
>
> —1 John 3:16

As the afternoon shadows melted into evening a young mother prepared dinner and then helped her children with their homework. The rest of the evening they watched television, then and the children settled into bed. With a deep sigh, the mother sat down with the latest novel, looking for the great escape. But painful thoughts intensified as she considered the perceived neglect by her husband—lack of money, no help with the house or the children.

The feelings of that long ago honeymoon had faded. She concluded that her husband no longer loved her. She thought, *I have made the worse mistake of my life.*

The next day she loaded up the children and a few clothes and drove to her parents' home. Her wise mother listened with an understanding heart. As the days went by, the older woman introduced positive thoughts and ideas that displaced the negative image the young wife held of her husband.

Gradually, these words began to take root, and in the mind of the young wife she began forming a positive image of her husband. After one of the numerous phone calls from her husband, she loaded the children into the car for their return trip. Today, in their retirement years this couple is enjoying

their grandchildren and great-grandchildren. Their relationship continues to grow.

What held this marriage together? It was not the love portrayed on television, in the theater, and in movies. Love is not about feelings; love is commitment. Love is a man and woman aligning themselves with one another. Keep Christ as the center of your marriage. Since the Holy Spirit has poured out God's love into our hearts—let us love one another even as we love ourselves.

A marriage takes work: learning good communication skills (which includes listening), assuming responsibility, forgiving and appreciating one another. Pray together, make room for each other to grow spiritually, and be thankful for one another.

> Fix your thoughts on what is true and good and right.
> Think about things that are pure and lovely, and dwell
> on the fine, good things in others…and be glad.
>
> —PHILIPPIANS 4:8, TLB

Daily Prayer

> *Father, we pray that the institution of marriage will be strengthened and regarded as holy unto the Lord. May husbands and wives rejoice and delight themselves in one another. We pray that they will learn to function so that each preserves individuality while responding to the desires of each other. This unity of persons is a mystery, but that is how it is when two people are united in Christ. So we pray that each will love and honor the other, and that they will let the miracle keep happening! In the name of Jesus, we pray. Amen.*

Day 4

Bestowing Generational Blessings

Daily Scripture Verse

> There is one who speaks like the piercings of a sword,
> But the tongue of the wise promotes health.
>
> —Proverbs 12:18

To minister effectively to the lives He has placed in your care, you must be cognizant of your influence. Much too often parents gossip, criticize, judge, and speak disparagingly of others, even to each other in the baby's hearing, not realizing that this child's memory is recording not only the words but also the attitudes and behaviors of the adults around him. What are you storing in your heart? Out of the abundance of the heart the mouth speaks.

The greatest gift you can give your baby is a love for God's Word. Remember, you are teaching your little one every day—he is watching you and listening to every word you speak. Speak words of wisdom commending knowledge that will enable your child to develop strength of character (Prov. 15:2). Always acknowledge the Holy Spirit; He is your divine helper, and He will bring to your remembrance the wisdom of God that you need for the moment and for the occasion.

Embrace wisdom, speak words of life, and proclaim the blessings of God in your child's hearing. Watch your words and hold your tongue; you'll save yourself a lot of grief (Prov. 21:23).

Someone has said, "The hand that rocks the cradle rules the world." Mother, you are usually the primary caregiver during your child's first six years. I pray that you will speak with wisdom and that faithful instruction shall be on your tongue.

Dad, build your child's self-esteem by telling her how blessed you are to have a daughter as wonderful as she is. A positive self-esteem and positive reinforcement begin with you. You are the hero, the one they look to for protection and leadership. Jesus has been made unto you wisdom.

> Now also when I am old and grayheaded,
> O God, do not forsake me,
> Until I declare Your strength to this generation,
> Your power to everyone who is to come.
> —PSALM 71:18

Daily Prayer

> *Our Father, Your kingdom come, Your will be done in our families even as it is in heaven; hallow Your name in our families. You chose us before the foundation of the world, and we thank You for pouring out Your Spirit upon our offspring and Your blessings upon our descendants. You are contending with those who contend with us, and You are giving safety to our children and easing them day-by-day. Thank You for forgiving all our iniquities, healing all our diseases, and crowning us with loving-kindness and tender mercies, in the name of Jesus. Amen.*

Day 5

What to Do When Your Child Goes Astray

Daily Scripture Verse

> And these words which I command you today shall be in your heart. You shall teach them diligently to your children, and shall talk of them when you sit in your

house, when you walk by the way, when you lie down, and when you rise up.

—Deuteronomy 6:6–7

The Word of God declares that parents have been given an awesome responsibility, but much too often we fail. Many have married to get needs met and hurts healed; we hope that our fresh new spouse will resolve the issues from our past. We are disappointed and frustrated when we discover they are looking to us with the same expectations. With our unmet needs, unhealed hurts, and unresolved issues we begin having children.

Our spiritual journey becomes difficult and more painful when a child goes astray. Here we are with answers to their problems at last, but they don't seem to hear us. We pay for rehab, seek help from the psychiatrist, counselor, psychologist, and friends. We blame teachers, society, the church, the other parent, and ourselves. In fact, in our ignorance, we often reinforce their rebellion against God.

We become emotionally distraught, and our emotions get in the way of answered prayer. We struggle with anger, guilt, remorse, regret, resentment, and unforgiveness. We try bribes and manipulation, and we exercise control tactics with shattering results. We take the decisions of our children personally and give Satan more tools to separate, divide, and conquer. Satan intensifies our *ifs*—"if only I had done this or not done that."

The Bible is about relationships—relationship with God and relationship with man. The Bible addresses marital relationships, parent-child relationships, employer-employee relationships, friendships, and how to relate to our enemies.

The children of God are called the family of God. He is our Father—our Father who is in heaven. The Father has given His name to the entire family—both in heaven and on earth. We must be strengthened in the depths of our being by the Spirit.

It seems this is the foundation for our relationships. He prays that we will be able to trust to the degree that Christ will be able to be at home in us, and we will be rooted and grounded in love. Without love we are nothing.

> Though I speak with the tongues of men and of angels, but have not love, I have become sounding brass or a clanging cymbal. And though I have the gift of prophecy, and understand all mysteries and all knowledge, and though I have all faith, so that I could remove mountains, but have not love, I am nothing.
>
> —1 Corinthians 13:1–2

Daily Prayer

> *Heavenly Father, my household and I shall be saved because I believe on the Lord Jesus. Thank You for choosing us before the foundation of the world. Every member of my household is accepted in the Beloved, the Lord Jesus Christ. You give abundant water for my thirst and for my parched fields. Thank You for pouring out Your Spirit and Your blessings on my children, in the name of Jesus. Amen.*

Day 1

Don't Abuse Your Liberty

Daily Scripture Verse

> For you, brethren, have been called to liberty; only do not use liberty as an opportunity for the flesh, but through love serve one another. For all the law is fulfilled in one word, even in this: "You shall love your neighbor as yourself."
>
> —GALATIANS 5:13–14

God called us to freedom and commanded us not to abuse our liberty. When we use it as an excuse to satisfy our selfish desires, we hurt each other. If we continue tearing each other apart we will completely destroy ourselves.

What are we teaching our children about freedom? We need a clear definition of freedom from a biblical perspective. Freedom is more than a right; it is a gift from God. Jesus gave Himself for our sins to free us from this present evil world (Gal. 1:4). God gave us grace and peace, freeing us from fears, agitating passions, and moral conflicts (1 Pet. 1:2).

With freedom comes the responsibility of walking uprightly, and freedom affords us the opportunity to worship God and fulfill our responsibility as reliable, solid citizens. True human freedom comes only from God and requires obedience. "Let every soul be subject to the governing authorities. For there is no authority except from God, and the authorities that exist are appointed by God. Therefore whoever resists the authority resists the ordinance of God, and those who resist will bring judgment on themselves" (Rom. 13:1–2).

Abusing our freedom through disobedience brings restriction and can even lead to death. The lives of individuals will

change when we exchange selfish desires for the precepts of a loving God. We can't begin too early teaching our children to speak truly, deal truly, and live truly. Jesus said that you shall know the truth, and the truth shall make you free (John 8:32).

Daily Prayer

> *Father, in the name of Jesus, we ask You to provide for and protect the families of our armed forces. Preserve marriages; cause the hearts of the parents to turn toward their children and the hearts of the children to turn toward the fathers and mothers. I plead the blood of Jesus (divine protection) over our troops and their families. Provide a support system to undergird, uplift, and edify those who have been left to raise children alone. Through Your Holy Spirit, comfort the lonely and strengthen the weary, in the name of Jesus. Amen.[21]*

Day 2

Spiritual Freedom Is Costly

Daily Scripture Verse

> Therefore take heed to yourselves and to all the flock, among which the Holy Spirit has made you overseers, to shepherd the church of God which He purchased with His own blood.
>
> —Acts 20:28

Freedom is costly; it is not free. Jesus gave His life to give us spiritual freedom, and many have died to obtain and maintain our national freedom—freedom to worship God and serve one another. John Adams wrote concerning the Declaration of Independence, "I am well aware of the toil and blood and treasure

that it will cost us to maintain this Declaration, and support and defend these States. Yet through all the gloom I can see rays of ravishing light and glory. I can see that the end is worth more than all the means."[22]

Let us bless our children and teach them to cherish and preserve freedom of spirit. Freedom is God's will, and their responsibility is to walk uprightly before Him. Our children are our future, and we must give them hope for tomorrow by teaching them truth that will make them free to carry the banner of freedom and enjoy glorious liberty. May future generations see the bright rays of *ravishing light and glory* burning throughout our land *with freedom's holy light*, manifesting to the world God's eternal love.

> For this is the will of God, that by doing good you may put to silence the ignorance of foolish men—as free, yet not using liberty as a cloak for vice, but as bondservants of God. Honor all people. Love the brotherhood. Fear God. Honor the king.
> —1 Peter 2:15–17

Daily Prayer

Heavenly Father, thank You for my country, the United States of America, the only country in the world founded upon religious freedom and Your Word. Thank You for our Founding Fathers, Lord, who looked to You for guidance to develop the kind of government that would be pleasing to You. We need Your wisdom to safeguard our freedom. May the light of Your Word run swiftly throughout our country, and may Your love burn brightly in our land. Give us a rebirth of freedom, in the name of Jesus. Amen.

Prayers That Avail Much* *for* Daily Living ❧ Germaine Copeland

Day 3

Are We Teaching Our Children the Truth About Freedom?

Daily Scripture Verse

> For you were bought at a price, therefore glorify God
> in your body and in your spirit, which are God's.
> —1 CORINTHIANS 6:20

Overseas our country was at war fighting for freedom from tyranny. Here at home my schoolmates and I reverently sang, "America, America…" After much bloodshed, our military troops returned home at the end of World War II celebrating, and we believed in brotherhood and freedom. With boldness, gratitude, and hope we pledged allegiance to the United States of America, believing every word. At public gatherings everyone sang the national anthem with great pride and maybe a tear in his eye.

Around the world we were respected and known as Christian America. In our country anyone who worked hard could achieve the Great American Dream. In their book *The Light and the Glory*, Peter Marshall and David Manuel wrote, "In general, we were the most steadying influence on an uneasy globe."

What happened to America? Does liberty give us permission to behave without regulations? It appears that to many in our society it means permissiveness—the right to do whatever we choose without interference from others.

Use your God-given opportunity—and responsibility—as a parent to teach your children the price of freedom. Help them to understand the enormous price paid by God Himself in the gift of His Son, Jesus, to die on a cross of shame to purchase our

salvation. Teach them about the price already paid by thousands and thousands of American men and women to keep our great nation free. Charge them to protect our nation's liberty—their own personal liberty—by living lives that honor God and country. Let freedom reign!

> But now having been set free from sin, and having become slaves of God, you have your fruit to holiness, and the end, everlasting life.
>
> —ROMANS 6:22

Daily Prayer

> *Father, Your Spirit has anointed us to change our world! Help us to be imitators of You and to bring good news to the poor and healing to the brokenhearted. Give us loving hearts so we will share Your love, which brings freedom to those in bondage and releases those who are oppressed. We make it our goal to bring refreshing to others, and we are refreshed! In Jesus' name we pray. Amen.*

Day 4

Women and Freedom

Daily Scripture Verse

> Charm is deceitful and beauty is passing,
> But a woman who fears the LORD, she shall be
>   praised.
> Give her of the fruit of her hands,
> And let her own works praise her in the gates.
>
> —PROVERBS 31:30–31

As I thumbed through a Christian magazine I was reminded of the thousands of women who are attending conventions across our land. We are packing auditoriums listening to charismatic leaders who are bringing us powerful, exciting messages of hope. Joyce Meyer, Anne Graham Lotz, Beth Moore, Paula White, Juanita Bynum, Cindy Jacobs, Barbara Wentroble, and many others are influencing our society.

Some are going into dangerous places, taking the message of deliverance to women of other nations. Women of other nations are experiencing the unconditional love of a loving Father. How do we maintain our deliverance, our freedom in Christ? Deliverance and salvation are the beginning to an intimate relationship with the Creator of the universe. God has made us strong. How are we using our strengths? We have a God-given intuition that comes from our innermost being. This ability is often turned into suspicion, disabling its function.

Woman is a threat to the kingdom of darkness. For centuries religion and society have imposed and reinforced a sense of guilt and condemnation on woman that goes back to the Garden of Eden. In Genesis 3:15, God spoke to the serpent, saying, "And I will put enmity between you and the woman, and between your seed and her Seed; He [Jesus] shall bruise your head, and you shall bruise His heel [harassing His body]."

Satan is our enemy. He will do anything he can to get us to follow his evil, deadly path. The phrase "you will bruise His heel" refers to Satan's repeated attempts to defeat Christ during His life on earth. "He will crush your head" foreshadows Satan's defeat when Christ rose from the dead. A strike on the heel is not deadly, but a crushing blow to the head is. Already God was revealing His plan to defeat Satan and offer salvation to the world through His Son, Jesus Christ.

Psalm 68:11 reveals that the Lord gave the word of power,

and He has called His women to bear and publish the Good News, and we are a great host! As we become more intimately acquainted with God through His Word and prayer, we assume our place in the body of Christ.

> The Lord gave the word;
> Great was the company of those who proclaimed it.
> —PSALM 68:11

Daily Prayer

Father, direct my steps by Your Word and let no iniquity have dominion over me. Uphold my steps in Your paths that my footsteps may not slip. Thank You that I am ever learning, ever growing, and ever achieving. Things change because I'm changing; I am wonderfully and fearfully made. You give me the freedom and courage to be my creative self, which You made unique unto me. In the name of Jesus I pray. Amen.

Day 5

Conformed to His Image

Daily Scripture Verse

For whom he did foreknow, he also did predestinate to be conformed to the image of his Son, that he might be the firstborn among many brethren.

—ROMANS 8:29, KJV

There was a time when self-hatred and self-abandonment controlled my thoughts and behavior. To be loved and accepted I had to be perfect, never make a mistake, never let others know the "real me."

For many years I perceived God as a cruel taskmaster with a heavy stick in His big hand waiting for me to mess up. He sent floods, lightning, and serpents to destroy those who didn't keep His commandments. He would even cause the ground to open up and swallow us. It seemed that I was always doing something wrong. At the age of seventeen, I attended my first movie, praying between nervous, raucous laughter that Jesus wouldn't split the eastern skies while I was in the den of iniquity. I just knew I would go straight to hell. I was so afraid of this God that I had carved out of the Old Testament stories.

My church taught perfectionism, and I worked hard to be conformed to the image of God's dear Son. But when I would climb one ladder of perfectionism, there was another ladder stacked on top of that one, and, heaving an anguished sigh, I would begin all over again. Finally, I became weary with trying, gave up, and decided that God had made a mistake. BUT GOD! He opened my blinded eyes—once I was blind, but now I see.

God has sent the Holy Spirit to take the things of Jesus and reveal them to us. When you read your Bible in communion with the Holy Spirit, you become more intimately acquainted with Jesus. To know Jesus is to know the Father. You can know the true God, a loving Father. He chose you before the foundation of the world to be His very own child. You no longer have to be afraid to let others see the real you, the person God created you to be.

> But whoever did want him,
>> who believed he was who he claimed
>> and would do what he said,
> He made to be their true selves,
>> their child-of-God selves.
>
> —JOHN 1:12, THE MESSAGE

Daily Prayer

Father, in the name of Jesus, I thank You for redeeming me from the authority of darkness and translating me into the kingdom of Your dear Son. Once I was darkness, but now I am light; once I was blind, but now I can see. I loose old, corrupt perceptions about who You are, and bind my thought patterns to truth that makes me free. Today and every day, I submit to the constant ministry of transformation by the Holy Spirit. You are my God, and I will praise You! Amen.

Day 1

The Holy Spirit and You

Daily Scripture Verse

Then you will know the truth, and the truth will set you free.

—JOHN 8:32, NIV

*A*ll my life, at least since I learned to read, I searched for truth—truth that would liberate me from the restraints of legalism. I thought that leaving the shelter of my parents' home would make me free, but the freedom I craved would require more than changing locations. It would take voluntary submission to the Person of the Holy Spirit.

No person can reveal who Jesus is. It takes a spiritual revelation from the heavenly Father. Jesus said that it was to our advantage for Him to go away: "For if I do not go away, the Helper will not come to you" (John 16:7).

How frightening it must have been for the disciples when Jesus told them that He had to leave them. Realizing their fear, He assured them that the Father would send them another Helper who would abide with them forever. Jesus identified Him as the Spirit of Truth. In fact, He said to the disciples, "You already know Him for He dwells with you, and will be in you" (John 14:17–18).

This same Holy Spirit is with us today, and He will take up His abode in the believer. This is a most humbling concept—the One who hovered over the face of the waters in the beginning abides in us. So often we think of the Holy Spirit as a substance, a divine influence, or, as one minister said, "Maybe He is an apparition like Casper the friendly ghost."

As we read about the Holy Spirit, we discover that He is a

personality sent from God. He searches all things—the deep things of God—and reveals them unto us. (See 1 Corinthians 2:10–11.) Welcome the Holy Spirit; He will commune with you and guide you into all truth. He will teach you with spiritual words (the Bible). He will bring to your remembrance all things that Jesus said before He ascended to the Father. He is here to glorify Jesus.

> But when the Comforter (Counselor, Helper, Advocate, Intercessor, Strengthener, Standby) comes, Whom I will send to you from the Father, the Spirit of Truth Who comes (proceeds) from the Father, He [Himself] will testify regarding Me.
>
> —JOHN 15:26, AMP

Daily Prayer

> *Holy Spirit, You are yearning over me, and I welcome You to the glory of the Father. I am living the life of the Spirit, because You really dwell within me—You are directing and controlling me, and I am truly a child of God. Thank You for leading me into all truth. You are my counselor and teacher, my constant companion.*

Day 2

Controlled by the Holy Spirit

Daily Scripture Verse

> So that the righteous and just requirement of the Law might be fully met in us who live and move not in the ways of the flesh but in the ways of the Spirit [our lives governed not by the standards and according to

the dictates of the flesh, but controlled by the Holy Spirit].

—ROMANS 8:4, AMP

Walking very carefully, I made sure that I kept the brimming cup of hot tea steady and well balanced. Knowing that the slightest tilt would cause an overflow, I didn't take my eyes off the brimming cup. For the next several moments that mug controlled how I walked and commanded my full attention.

That beautiful mug became a symbol of an earthen vessel filled to the brim with the Word of God, a symbol of my own life—my cup was running over. The Holy Spirit is not pushy or demanding. He waits for me to submit to His control. I submit to His control according to the level of the Word I have received with understanding.

The Word is spiritual milk, meat—the Bread of Life. Jesus cleanses us by the washing of water with the Word. We can be filled with the Word—or filled with our own worries, fears, concerns, heartaches, resentment, unforgiveness, and woes.

When you are full of the Word, the Holy Spirit helps you—controlling how you talk and how you walk. The Word is God—God is love. Make a decision to really come to know, through experience, the love of Christ, which far surpasses mere knowledge. Then you will be filled through all your being unto all the fullness of God. Purpose to have the richest measure of His divine presence, and become a body wholly filled and flooded with God Himself. (See Ephesians 3:19.) Fill your heart and mind with words of life, "for out of the fullness (the overflow, the superabundance) of the heart the mouth speaks. The good man from his inner good treasure flings forth good things" (Matt. 12:34–35, AMP).

The fuller the vessel and the more your actions are controlled by the Holy Spirit, the more of God you experience.

I will take the cup of salvation, and call upon the name of the LORD.

—PSALM 116:13, KJV

Daily Prayer

Lord, Your Word says that we are to be holy to You, because You are holy, and You have set us apart to be Yours. Lord, thank You for choosing us as your treasured possessions. You live in us, and walk among us. You are our God, and we are Your people, the sheep of Your pasture. We are running over with thanksgiving because You are our Father, and we are Your sons and daughters. We will keep our way pure by reading and living according to Your Word, in the name of Jesus. Amen.

Day 3

The Filling Station

Daily Scripture Verse

In the secret place of Your presence You hide them from the plots of men; You keep them secretly in Your pavilion from the strife of tongues.

—PSALM 31:20, AMP

In the early fifties I first heard the great gospel singer Mahalia Jackson. I became an instant fan and acquired all the albums she had recorded at that time. As Mahalia sang, I would really get caught up in her soulful expressions of joy. Her heart was in her singing, and her singing was for the glory of God.

When she sang, "I found the answer, I learned to pray," you knew she had been with Jesus. She conveyed that message straight from the heart, telling in song her connection with God in prayer and her faith to guide her along the way.

She shared a story about her life, which was very heart-warming. Mahalia traveled to most of her concerts by automobile. There were times when the rigors of the road and the pressures of life made weariness her companion. She felt depleted and empty, physically and emotionally. She constantly poured herself into others and had very little time to replenish her spirit.

When the need came to withdraw from the circuit, she would go back to her home in Chicago for a few days of quiet meditation and communion with God. She would go down to the little church that she had attended in earlier years. She said, "I go to that little church and pray, and I feast on the Word and have fellowship with the brethren. It is my filling station. I go there to fill up when my body is tired, my mind is weary, and I need a refreshing from the Lord. Yes, I go to my filling station, away from the hustle and bustle and into my hiding place."

We also need to go to the "filling station" often. Your filling station can be getting alone with God, communing with Him, filling your mind and heart with the Word. It can be assembling with the brethren where, in the corporate anointing, you have your spirit filled to overflowing. It can be just loving God and telling Him how very much you need Him to be number one in your life.[23]

> Blessed are they which do hunger and thirst after righteousness: for they shall be filled.
>
> —MATTHEW 5:6, KJV

> *Heavenly Father, today I am singing a new song. Yesterday with its victories and failures has passed away, and behold, on this day all things have become new. I look forward to all things that You send my way—a new sunrise, new friends, relationships, assignments, responsibilities, blessings, and new opportunities to be a blessing to someone today. I release the past and will not judge by the former thought patterns and attitudes. Thank You, Lord Jesus, for Your goodness to me. The earth is full of God's unfailing love. Amen.*

Day 4

One Word From God Can Change Your Life

Daily Scripture Verse

> The Lord is near to all who call on him,
>> to all who call on him in truth.
>
> —PSALM 145:18, NIV

ev. Griffin's face was a mask of despair and unhappiness. He had preached every sermon he had carved out of the Scriptures, and preached everything he had heard others preach. Feeling bruised and weary beyond expression, he stood before the altar with the sunlight splashing through the stained-glass windows making patterns on the floor.

Alone in the church, he looked up past the vaulted ceiling, and with his voice rumbling like the roar of the ocean, he prayed: "God, after all these years, I still do not know what faith is. I have saturated my mind with Your Word, memorized large portions of Scripture, and repeated it over and over. I am so tired

of preaching the same messages Sunday after Sunday, year after year. It has all become words, a job that I do by rote. I can't go on like this." The Holy Spirit was searching his heart and the heart of another who would bring the answer from God.

Turning away from the splashes of sunlight, he walked away from the altar and out the door into the cold, brisk wintry wind. Pulling his overcoat around him, he walked back to the parsonage where he would prepare for the next day's worship service. Thoughts whirled: what would he tell his wife? What would he do about a job and a place to live? He had accumulated a few possessions over the years, but he had never owned a home.

One word from God changed this minister's life, and he was never the same. At the close of the service the next morning, a stranger walked up to Rev. Griffin. He had just returned to the States from South Africa. "Sir, God has heard your cry, and He sent me here this morning to give you these Bible lessons."

The Holy Spirit sent someone from another country to give this minister hope. Everything he had believed and preached was challenged, and he sought God with a fervor he had never known before. Faith became tangible, the old despair and boredom passed away, and for the first time ever he passionately spoke about the Father in an intimate, joyful tone. His preaching was charged with a new anointing, and those who heard him knew that he had been with Jesus.

> And he who searches our hearts knows the mind of the Spirit, because the Spirit intercedes for the saints in accordance with God's will.
>
> —ROMANS 8:27, NIV

Daily Prayer

> *Jesus, You are my Lord. You are my light and my salvation; I shall not be afraid. You are my sufficiency, my*

redeemer, provider, sanctifier, protector, healer, and victory! You are El Shaddai. You are more than enough for every challenge I face, for every decision I must make, for the questions I need answered, for the adjustments I need to make. You are everything to me, my Lord and Savior. I trust You, lean and rely on You. Lord, You are good; my refuge and counsel are in You. Amen.

Day 5

Strip Off the Old, and Put On the New

Daily Scripture Verse

Don't become so well-adjusted to your culture that you fit into it without even thinking. Instead, fix your attention on God. You'll be changed from the inside out. Readily recognize what he wants from you, and quickly respond to it. Unlike the culture around you, always dragging you down to its level of immaturity, God brings the best out of you, develops well-formed maturity in you.

—ROMANS 12:2, THE MESSAGE

*B*eing born again is the beginning of a brand-new life. Our spirit man is now a partaker of the divine nature of God. But before we can put on this new nature, the mind has to be renewed to the Word of God. Otherwise, the unsurrendered soul tries to hang on to its old life—it doesn't want to give up control.

In the earliest stages of my prayer life, I had no understanding about "stripping" away my former nature, so I ignored that part and skipped down to "putting on" the new. I can assure you

from personal experience that when your heart is upright before God, He moves heaven and earth to give you revelation knowledge with spiritual wisdom and understanding.

A few years ago, while driving down the highway near my home, overwhelming feelings of anger and confusion broke through my facade. "God," I prayed, "what's wrong with me? How dare I even think that I have anything spiritual to give to anyone? I cannot continue in ministry unless You do something to change me!"

When I stopped whining and complaining, the Lord said, "I am ready to help you work out your salvation by working into your inner being all that you have prayed to be established in others."

God's Word revealed some wrong attitudes and negative thought patterns. It exposed, sifted, and analyzed the very thoughts and intents of my heart, which had long lain in a sea of forgetfulness. As it turned out I had forgotten a past that had not forgotten me. Together, the Holy Spirit and I began to strip away, put off, and discard my old unrenewed self. This was the beginning of a painful but rewarding new life.

The unsurrendered soul, with its spoiled virtue and cancerous garbage, had to give way to the planted Word of God, which saves the soul (James 1:21, NIV). Old thought patterns and attitudes are replaced with God's thoughts, and the love of God, which is shed abroad in our hearts, drives out the streaks of selfishness, making way for us to walk in paths of righteousness.

> Strip yourselves of your former nature [put off and discard your old unrenewed self] which characterized your previous manner of life and becomes corrupt through lusts and desires that spring from delusion; and be constantly renewed in the spirit of your mind

[having a fresh mental and spiritual attitude], and put on the new nature (the regenerate self) created in God's image, [Godlike] in true righteousness and holiness.

—EPHESIANS 4:22–24, AMP

Daily Prayer

Father, I affirm the lordship of Jesus over my everyday life. When I was a child, I talked, thought, and reasoned like a child. I strip off the old thought patterns as they are exposed. The blood of Christ purges my conscience from dead works of selfishness, agitating passions, and moral conflicts. Holy Spirit, help me grow up in every way, speaking truly, dealing truly, and living truly. Jesus is Lord over my spirit, soul, and body. Amen.

Day 1

Prayer Bells Are Ringing

Daily Scripture Verse

> But as for me, I will come into your Temple protected by your mercy and your love; I will worship you with deepest awe.
>
> —PSALM 5:7, TLB

*D*o you hear the ringing of the prayer bells? The Father is waiting in the prayer tower of your soul, waiting and longing to have a talk with you. He wants you to know Him as intimately as the Old Testament prophets knew Him. You can confidently enter the most holy place by the blood of Jesus. (See Hebrews 10:19.) He is the way to the Father.

Moses, an Old Testament prophet, knew God, and he knew the ways of God. He was not afraid to reveal his disappointments, frustrations, anger, and fears to the God in whose presence he dwelled. David, who wrote many of the psalms, expressed his innermost thoughts to Jehovah God even while declaring his trust in Him. In Lamentations 3:17, the prophet Jeremiah expressed his true feelings of despair. This opened the door for him to receive hope and confidence.

You can talk openly with God—your wonderful Counselor, your Prince of Peace—about anything. Tell Him your innermost thoughts. Describe your fondest dreams. Expose your true feelings, desires, wants, and needs. Express your love and gratitude to Him with thanksgiving. It may be possible to hide your true feelings from others or even from yourself, but it is impossible to hide your feelings from God.

Often feelings are a barometer, alerting us to a need for change in our thought life and attitudes. Unfortunately, we

sometimes misuse the Scriptures as a cover-up for a feeling we perceive as *wrong* instead of acknowledging the feeling and expecting answers from the Lord to determine the cause and the remedy. God is concerned about everything that concerns you (Ps. 138:8). Ask Him for what you believe you need. Allow Him the time to speak to you and to show you your *real* need.

> [God's] compassion never ends. It is only the Lord's mercies that have kept us from complete destruction. Great is his faithfulness; his loving-kindness begins afresh each day.
>
> —LAMENTATIONS 3:22–23, TLB

Daily Prayer

> *Lord, You are my strength and my shield; my heart trusts in You, and I am helped. My heart leaps for joy, and I will give thanks to You. Thank You for arming me with strength and making my way perfect. In the name of Jesus, I can face challenges with wisdom, understanding, intelligence, and supernatural ability because Your Word dwells in me richly. I can do all things through Christ who strengthens me. In the name of Jesus, I pray. Amen.*

Day 2

Praise Him in the Secret Place

Daily Scripture Verse

> From the lips of children and infants
>   you have ordained praise
> because of your enemies,
>   to silence the foe and the avenger.
>
> —PSALM 8:2, NIV

The psalmist David would talk to himself during times of discouragement: "Why am I discouraged? Why so sad?" Then he would declare his trust in God. "I will put my hope in God! I will praise him again—my Savior and my God!" (Ps. 42:11, nlt).

Talk with God by praising Him for answered prayer and for your victories and successes. Then thank Him for all He has provided for you. He created you. He understands you, and He can *fix* you when you submit to His instruction. He binds up and heals your wounded soul, takes the sting out of painful memories, dissolves your toxic shame, and gives you the grace to overcome your fears and failures.

God desires to meet with you, to hear your voice, and to see your face before Him. So come into the holy of holies and receive His love, His healing, His mercy, and His grace. Great is His faithfulness!

God can be trusted with your secrets. He will never betray you. He is the God who hears and answers prayer.

> My dove in the clefts of the rock,
> > in the hiding places on the mountainside,
> show me your face,
> > let me hear your voice;
> for your voice is sweet,
> > and your face is lovely.
> —SONG OF SOLOMON 2:14, NIV

Daily Prayer

Most Holy God, thank You! Everything in me says, "Thank You!" Thank You for Your love, thank You for Your faithfulness. Most holy is Your name, most holy is Your Word. The moment I called out, You stepped in, and You made my life large with strength. You began a

*good work in me, and I thank You for helping me grow
in grace until Your task within me is finally finished on
that day when Jesus Christ returns. Your Word equips
me for every good work—to do good to everyone, in the
name of Jesus. Amen.*

Day 3

Healing in the Secret Place

Daily Scripture Verse

> But he was pierced for our transgressions,
>   he was crushed for our iniquities;
> the punishment that brought us peace was upon him,
>   and by his wounds we are healed.
>
> —ISAIAH 53:5, NIV

Acknowledging your emotional pain positions you to receive healing and restoration. His grace enables you to forgive those who have harmed you and to forgive yourself for harming others, allowing you to make amends when necessary. You are able to comfort others with the comfort you have received.

This kind of honesty with ourselves and with God enables us, with the assistance of the Holy Spirit, to clear out emotional interference to an effective prayer life. David understood this when he prayed as he did in Psalm 51.

The blood of Jesus washes us and cleanses us. As we proclaim scriptural prayers over our own lives and the lives of others, the Word of God creates in us a pure heart, renews a steadfast spirit within us, restores to us the joy of His salvation, and grants us a willing spirit to sustain us. Then we are able to teach

transgressors His ways, and sinners will turn back to Him. (See Psalm 51:7–13.)

> Who can discern his errors?
> > Forgive my hidden faults.
> Keep your servant also from willful sins;
> > may they not rule over me.
> Then will I be blameless,
> > innocent of great transgression.
>
> —Psalm 19:12–13, niv

Daily Prayer

To You, O Lord, I pray. My enemies will not triumph over me, and I will never be disgraced for trusting You. Show me the path where I should go; point out the right road for me to walk. Lead and teach me, for You are the God who gives me salvation. Thank You for seeing me through eyes of everlasting love and kindness. Your integrity and uprightness will preserve me, in the name of Jesus. Amen.

Day 4

The Adventure of Prayer

Daily Scripture Verse

Also [Jesus] told them a parable to the effect that they ought always to pray and not to turn coward (faint, lose heart, and give up).

> —Luke 18:1, amp

*H*onesty with God and with yourself is the best policy. It is the only pathway to effective intercessory prayer. God

will not allow you to control or manipulate another person's will. But when you are in right fellowship with God and with others, your prayers influence people and bring them to the moment of truth where they can receive the motivating knowledge to make a decision on their own. God has called us to be laborers together with Him, and He involves us in His plan of salvation as His instruments of righteousness to pray for His will to be done on earth even as it is in heaven.

Developing a consistent prayer life is an adventure in faith. God is very practical, and He has reserved specific pathways of prayer for you to walk as you become more deeply and intimately acquainted with Him.

You will have experiences as you move from one degree of glory to another. However, be careful not to seek sensationalism or attempt to reproduce in the flesh the experiences you had in the Spirit. Seeking experiences opens the door for demonic activity fabricated by familiar spirits. These spirits use our misguided thought patterns to keep us unbalanced and prevent us from pursuing an intimate relationship with God our Father.

One of our greatest temptations is to place God in a box. We want Him to answer our prayers in the exact manner He did previously. How we love formulas with steps 1, 2, and 3! But we must never forget that God is a multifaceted God. He answers prayer in His own way and in His timing. He may not answer when you want Him to, but He will always answer on time.

> So let us come boldly to the very throne of God and stay there to receive his mercy and to find grace to help us in our times of need.
> —Hebrews 4:16, TLB

> *Heavenly Father, I repent of my thoughts, words, and actions that have been unlike You. Cleanse me with the blood of Jesus. Renew and transform me as I daily read and meditate on Your Word. Thank You for sending a refreshing to my whole spirit, soul, and body as I spend time in Your presence. The power of the life-giving Spirit—power that is mine through Christ Jesus—has freed me from the vicious circle of sin and death. Today, I am anointed with fresh oil from the Holy Spirit. In the name of Jesus, amen.*

Day 5

The Prayer Tower

Daily Scripture Verse

> The Lord is my rock, and my fortress, and my deliverer; my God, my strength, in whom I will trust; my buckler, and the horn of my salvation, and my high tower.
>
> —Psalm 18:2, kjv

We often insist that God do things at our level of understanding when He wants to lead us to higher heights and deeper depths. Demanding that He perform His works exactly as He did in our last encounter with Him hinders our spiritual development and cuts off answers to our prayers.

Our God knows every aspect of every situation, and He continually desires to teach us His higher thoughts and His ways. Choose to walk the high road where the prayer bells are ringing. Take time to rest at the prayer tower and have a talk

with the Father in the name of Jesus. "He will hear your faintest cry, and I He will answer bye and bye."[24]

> As the heavens are higher than the earth,
>> so are my ways higher than your ways
>> and my thoughts than your thoughts.
>
> —ISAIAH 55:9, NIV

Daily Prayer

Father, I thank You for the Holy Spirit who brings all things to my remembrance. As far as I am concerned, Father God, You turn to good what is meant for evil. You brought me to the position I hold today for the benefit of others. I rest in You knowing that in all things You are working for my good because I love You, and You called me according to Your purpose. I will trust in You, Lord, at all times for Your ways are perfect. In Jesus' name, I pray. Amen.

Day 1

A Celebration of Life

Daily Scripture Verse

> He is not here; for He is risen, as He said. Come, see
> the place where the Lord lay. And go quickly and tell
> His disciples that He is risen from the dead.
>
> —MATTHEW 28:6–7

*J*esus is alive! He is not a myth or a fairy tale. He lives; I know
He lives. He is my best friend and my elder brother. He is
the Son who rose with healing in His wings, my redeemer.

This was not always true for me. In my formative years, I
was taught a concept of Jesus, but He seemed far removed from
where I lived; how could I possibly trust someone I didn't know?
Easter meant an Easter egg hunt, chocolate bunnies, pretty
clothes, a day of pageantry at the church, and usually a sunrise
service.

Each spring just as the golden forsythia and jonquils
appeared, we were busy with extra choir rehearsals, and the
true meaning of this celebration escaped me. Who was this Person I did not understand? Did He really exist? The church gave
me rules and regulations, but did not give me answers to life's
enigmas, and my world grew more complex with the passage
of time.

The desire to understand the meaning of life and where
I was going became my motivation for living, but none of my
efforts made any difference—just wind blowing here and there,
but going nowhere. Having walked all the pathways of philosophy I read about, I decided to give God one more chance. I cried
out for truth—the truth and the wisdom of the ages.

One day while sitting at my kitchen table, radiant beams

filtered through the darkness of my soul, and the truth I had searched for appeared. My own resurrection morning dawned, changing my life for all time.

The true meaning of Easter is resurrection power that will turn your gloom to joy, your turmoil to peace, your depression to hope. Jesus will transform your life, give you a reason to live, show you the pathway of life, and help you become your true self. Truth is a Person. His name is Jesus.

And the LORD appeared unto him the same night....
—GENESIS 26:24

Daily Prayer

Hosanna! Blessed is He who comes in the name of the Lord! We shout with joy, for our King is coming! Jesus, You are the righteous one, the victor! Salvation now, GOD—a free and full life! We bless You out of the house of the Lord. We are the righteousness of God in Christ, and we will flourish like palm trees and grow tall like Lebanon cedars. Blessed is He who comes in the name of the Lord! Amen.

Day 2

Rejoice!

Daily Scripture Verse

Do not be afraid, for behold, I bring you good tidings of great joy which will be to all people. For there is born to you this day in the city of David a Savior, who is Christ the Lord.

—LUKE 2:10–11

*I*t is the middle of the night; ideas whirl around inside my head like bed sheets flapping and snapping on a clothesline in blustery weather. Snuggling in my bed, I try to ignore the accompanying worries yapping at my mind. Too early to get up, but sleep had taken its flight.

Turning on the light, I open *Prayers That Avail Much*. Reading aloud the scriptural written prayers, "Victory Over Depression," "Adoration," and "To Rejoice in the Lord," I shape all those worries and concerns into prayers of thanksgiving and praise. The raging winds stop and the voice of worry is hushed, replaced with joy unspeakable and full of glory.

Joy is more than a feeling. It is a fruit of the Spirit, which takes root within the re-created human spirit. It is God's will for your joy to be full. Joy is a valuable weapon of spiritual warfare.

You do not have to settle for less than God's fullness of joy. Jesus promised: "You'll be full of joy, and it will be a joy no one can rob from you" (John 16:22, THE MESSAGE). You are redeemed! The Word of God has been given to you so that your joy will be full. You can choose to be happy or unhappy. Thoughts of worry, defeat, and doubt will come, but you can turn them out of doors, cast them away by thinking on right things. Praying scriptural prayers aloud will quiet your mind and help you refocus.

Meditate on the Word of Truth, the goodness of God, His promises, His testimonies, His nature, His fullness, His authority, and His love, and rejoice; again I say, rejoice! The worries of this life will begin to drop off and be replaced with joy, confidence, and faith when you think on eternal things.

It is a most wonderful time of the year—a time of celebration because we rejoice in God's gift to us, His Son, Jesus Christ. Let the bells of your heart rejoice in prayers of thanksgiving with high-sounding praises. Let the trumpet of your voice announce

His praises. Open wide your mouth to shout and sing the truth of His Word: "Father, this is the day You have made. I rejoice, and I am glad in it! I rejoice in You always. And again I say, I rejoice!"

> Be glad in the LORD and rejoice, you righteous;
> And shout for joy, all you upright in heart!
>
> —PSALM 32:11

Daily Prayer

> *Wonderful counselor, mighty God, everlasting Father, Prince of Peace, You are my God, and I trust You. Today I bless those family members and friends with whom I will be interacting during this Christmas season. Father, through Jesus Christ, You have enriched us in every way—in all our speaking and in all knowledge. We will glory in Your love, thanking You that through the Holy Spirit we are strengthened and empowered in our innermost beings. We are learning of the height and depth of Your great love for us, in the name of Jesus. Amen.*

Day 3

A Christmas Message and Prayer

Daily Scripture Verse

> The LORD your God in your midst
> The Mighty One, will save;
> He will rejoice over you with gladness,
> He will quiet you with His love,
> He will rejoice over you with singing.
>
> —ZEPHANIAH 3:17

*I*t was Christmas time, and I was busy preparing for that glorious day when the children and grandchildren would be home. After Christmas brunch we would gather around the Christmas tree to open gifts. While looking over one of my many lists of things to do, I realized that something was missing—I forgot to pray.

Immediately I stood up and went to the piano where I began playing and singing spontaneous songs to Jesus, my Lord and Savior. As the music faded I began to weep; I said, "Lord, I've asked everyone what they want for Christmas except You. Forgive me for neglecting our time together. It is Your birthday we are celebrating. I've never asked before. I'm asking now: what do You want for Your birthday? Had You not come to earth, we wouldn't even have a special day we call Christmas. You are the wonder of all wonders. What do You desire?"

In the stillness of that moment, He answered me in a song of the Spirit. *All I want is You.* The words and music began to ascend as my heart was thrilled, "All I want is you, a living sacrifice, a friend, a lover, a sister, a brother. All I want is you."

What do you have to give this year? All He wants is you.

> Therefore, I urge you, brothers, in view of God's mercy, to offer your bodies as living sacrifices, holy and pleasing to God—this is your spiritual act of worship.
>
> —ROMANS 12:1, NIV

Daily Prayer

> *Heavenly Father, thank You for this beautiful Christmas Eve. Most of all I thank You for giving us Your Son, Jesus. Jesus, thank You for bearing our sins on the cross so that we can live unto righteousness, and by Your stripes we are healed. We bless You, Father, Son, and Holy Ghost. Tonight we will go to bed with great expectations, looking*

forward to celebrating with family and friends the birth of our Lord and Savior. Thank You for forgiving our sins and casting them into the depths of the sea, in the name of Jesus. Amen.[25]

Day 4

A Night to Remember (Part 1)

Daily Scripture Verse

And she brought forth her firstborn Son, and wrapped Him in swaddling cloths, and laid Him in a manger, because there was no room for them in the inn.

—LUKE 2:7

The night was cold when the innkeeper's wife awakened me. She gave me a stack of blankets and told me to take them to the young couple sleeping in the barn. With sleep-filled eyes I threw on my cloak and hurried across the backyard. I pushed hard against the great doors, and looking inside I saw the couple my master had almost turned away because there was no room in the hostel. Just as I was about to ask if they needed anything, I heard the sounds of a newborn baby.

Unsure about what to do, I was glad when Joseph beckoned me to come near. They were quietly praising God for the baby, and Mary said, "His name is Jesus." She looked at me with loving eyes and asked me for warm water, and together we bathed the newborn baby boy. With her assistance I wrapped Him in swaddling clothes, held Him for a few moments, and with a kiss I gently laid Him in the manger. There was something different about this baby. I felt washed inside and out. I felt brand-new, and I knew that I would never be the same.

A holy hush surrounded the place, and I decided to sleep in the stable in case they needed me for anything else. Without warning, we were awakened and saw several shepherds from the area. They all began talking at once about something strange and wonderful that happened in the fields where they were keeping their flocks by night.

Mary listened, as we all did, with rapt attention to the amazing things they were telling. It seemed that we were actually in the field with them. Suddenly, God's angel stood among them, and God's glory blazed all around. They were terrified until the angel said, "Don't be afraid. I'm here to announce a great and joyful event that is meant for everyone. A Savior has just been born in David's town, a Savior who is Messiah and Master. This is what you're to look for: a baby wrapped in a blanket and lying in a manger." They were thrilled that it was just as they had been told.

We envisioned the angelic choir singing God's praises. The shepherds said that they rejoiced as the angels sang, "Glory to God in the highest, and on earth peace, goodwill toward men."

My, it was a strange night. Joseph, Mary, and I were awestruck as the stable became crowded. Others who looked like wealthy traders from the East appeared saying they had followed a star to this very stable. They gave beautiful gifts to this special baby—the Son of God.

Darkness was pushed back as a brilliant light shone all around. Everyone reverently knelt to worship this baby that I held so close to my heart. Through tears of joy I thanked God for choosing me to hold the Messiah.

Glory to God in the highest,
And on earth peace, goodwill toward men!
—Luke 2:14

> *Father, we come to celebrate the gift that You sent to us,
> the birth of Jesus—Emmanuel, God with us. We pray
> that future generations will remember the sacred purpose
> of this celebration and follow in our footsteps as we follow
> You. Jesus, we acknowledge that You are the Word that
> became flesh and lived among us. You are full of grace
> and truth, and from You we receive one gift after another.
> I give You all that I have. I give You myself—spirit, soul,
> and body, and pray that future generations will walk in
> truth. Amen.*

Day 5

A Night to Remember (Part 2)

Daily Scripture Verse

> And Jesus increased in wisdom and stature, and in
> favor with God and men.
>
> —LUKE 2:52

The baby grew in stature and in wisdom. Jesus became a man who went about doing good, healing all those oppressed by the devil, and I became one of His disciples. He was the Word made flesh—He dwelt among us. I heard Him preach Good News to the multitudes that followed Him. He even fed them with a lad's lunch. He healed the sick and opened blind eyes, and I saw a crippled man walk. Winds and storms obeyed His command, and He raised the dead.

He called twelve apostles to work with Him in His ministry. Jesus honored women and restored them to a place of dignity. Mary Magdalene joined His company after He cast seven

demons out of her. One day when I was with Him I saw religious leaders surrounding a woman who was caught in adultery, and they were planning to stone her to death. Jesus saved her from the mob and forgave her sins. He actually talked to a Samaritan woman and forgave her. He did many miracles. He is my Lord. His name is wonderful Counselor, mighty God, everlasting Father, the Prince of Peace. He is the great I Am.

Have you met my Lord and Savior? He came to take away the sins of the world. He was bruised for our iniquities, the chastisement of our peace was upon Him, and by His stripes we are healed. Ask Him to come into your heart and forgive your sins. If you ask Him to be your Lord, He will save you, He will heal you, and He will be a present help in time of trouble. Jesus is the way to the Father.

December 25 is the day we have designated to celebrate the birth of Jesus. On this day and every day we will rejoice and generate joy unspeakable and full of glory. We rejoice because He is our exceeding great joy. We rejoice in the hope of the glory of God. We rejoice because Jesus came to earth, died, and rose again. The Lord reigns. Blessed be the name of the Lord!

> For the grace of God that brings salvation has appeared to all men, teaching us that...we should live soberly, righteously, and godly in the present age, looking for the blessed hope and glorious appearing of our great God and Savior Jesus Christ, who gave Himself for us.
>
> —TITUS 2:11–14

Daily Prayer

Father, this is eternal life that we may know You, the only true God, and Jesus Christ whom You have sent. I thank You for sending Jesus to earth; to know Him is to know

You. I thank You for the Holy Spirit who comforts and helps me—teaching me all things that You have said. I pause and take time to meditate on Your promises in the midst of my preparations for Christmas, in the name of Jesus. You are my strength, my light, and my salvation. Amen.

Notes

1. Excerpted from "To Walk in the Word," *Prayers That Avail Much* Commemorative Edition (Tulsa, OK: Harrison House, 1997). All rights reserved.

2. C. S. Lewis, *The Screwtape Letters* (New York: Harper SanFrancisco, 2001).

3. Hannah Hurnard, *Hinds' Feet on High Places* (Carol Stream, IL: Tyndale House Publishers, 1986).

4. Adapted from Women of Destiny Bible (Nashville, TN: Thomas Nelson, Inc., 2000).

5. Oswald Chambers, *My Utmost for His Highest Journal* (Uhrichsville, OH: Barbour Publishing, 1935), s.v. May 3. This edition published by special arrangements with and permission of Discovery House publishers. Copyright © 1935 by Dodd. Mead & Company, Inc. Copyright renewed 1963 by Oswald Chambers Publications Association, Ltd. All rights reserved.

6. You will be encouraged when you hear his message of the Father's love, and how God brought him to the place of decision. To order, please contact Word Ministries, Inc., 38 Sloan Street, Roswell, GA 30075. You may also call our offices 770-518-1065, or contact us at www.prayers.org.

7. Adapted from "Protection From Terrorism," *Prayers That Avail Much* Commemorative Edition (Tulsa, OK: Harrison House, 1997), 381. All rights reserved.

8. Excerpted from the prayer, "American Government," *Prayers That Avail Much* Commemorative Edition (Tulsa, OK: Harrison House, 1997), 393. All rights reserved.

9. David Yonggi Cho, *Prayer: Key to Revival* (Nashville, TN: Thomas Nelson, Inc., 1984).

10. E. W. Kenyon, *In His Presence*, 29th ed., (Lynnwood, WA: Kenyon Gospel Publishers, 1991).

11. Prayer adapted from "Handling the Day of Trouble or Calamity," *Prayers That Avail Much* Commemorative Gift Edition.

12.   "Where Could I Go" by James B. Coats. Copyright © 1940 Stamps, Baxter Music (admin. by Brentwood-Benson Music Publishing, Inc., 741 Coolsprings Blvd., Franklin TN 37067). Used by permission.

13.   This devotional entry was created by Lane Holland, who can be contacted by e-mail at: lane@prayers.org. Used by permission.

14.   Ibid.

15.   Ibid.

16.   Excerpted from "Giving Thanks to God," *Prayers That Avail Much*, vol. 3, 120.

17.   Kenyon, *In His Presence*.

18.   Excerpted from Germaine Copeland, *The Road God Walks* (Tulsa, OK: Harrison House Publishers, 2000).

19.   "O How I Love Jesus" by Frederick Whitfield. Public domain.

20.   Women of Destiny Bible, 3, adapted from Fuchsia Pickett, *God's Dream* (Shippensburg, PA: Destiny Image Publishers, 1991).

21.   *Prayers That Avail Much* Commemorative Edition, version for members of the Armed Forces.

22.   John Adams, letter to Abigail Adams, July 3, 1776, *Adams Family Correspondence*, ed. L. H. Butterfield, vol. 2, p. 31 (1963), http://www.bartleby.com/73/392 (accessed August 17, 2004).

23.   This devotional entry is used by permission of Margaret Bomar Minisries. Copyright © 2003.

24.   "Just a Little Talk With Jesus" by Cleavant Derricks, copyright © 1937, renewed 1965 by Stamps-Baxter Music (admin. by Brentwood-Benson Music Publishing, Inc., 741 Cool Springs Blvd., Franklin, TN 37067). Used by permission.

25.   Germaine Copeland, *Prayers That Avail Much*: First Blessings for Your Child (Lake Mary, FL: Charisma House, 2001).

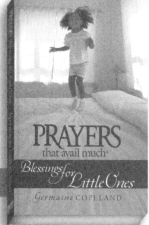

Strang Communications, the publisher of both Charisma House and *Charisma* magazine, wants to give you 3 FREE ISSUES of our award-winning magazine.

Since its inception in 1975, *Charisma* magazine has helped thousands of Christians stay connected with what God is doing worldwide.

Within its pages you will discover in-depth reports and the latest news from a Christian perspective, biblical health tips, global events in the body of Christ, personality profiles, and so much more. Join the family of *Charisma* readers who enjoy feeding their spirit each month with miracle-filled testimonies and inspiring articles that bring clarity, provoke prayer, and demand answers.

To claim your **3 free issues** of *Charisma,* send your name and address to: Charisma 3 Free Issue Offer, 600 Rinehart Road, Lake Mary, FL 32746. Or you may call 1-800-829-3346 and ask for Offer # 93FREE. This offer is only valid in the USA.

---

www.charismamag.com

3581